Penguin Pocket Wri

Martin H. Manser has been a professional reference-book editor since 1980. He received a BA Honours degree in linguistics at the conclusion of his studies at the universities of York, England, and Regensburg, Germany, and went on to gain an M.Phil. degree for research into the influence of English on modern German. A developing interest in lexicography led him to take up a post as a reference-book editor. Since 1980 he has worked on about one hundred reference books with a contemporary appeal. His English-language reference titles include the *Penguin Wordmaster Dictionary*, the Bloomsbury *Good Word Guide*, Chambers' *Dictionary of Synonyms and Antonyms*, the Macmillan *Student's Dictionary*, the Facts on File *Visual Dictionary*, the Oxford *Learner's Pocket Dictionary*, the Guinness *Book of Words*, the *New Penguin Thesaurus* and *The Wordsworth Crossword Companion* (with Stephen Curtis).

He has also compiled and edited many titles that encourage Bible reading, including the *NIV Thematic Study Bible* on which he was Managing Editor, (Hodder & Stoughton and Zondervan), the Hodder & Stoughton and Zondervan *Dictionary of Bible Themes*, *Bible Quotation Collection* (Lion), *The Christian Quotation Collection* (Westminster John Knox), the *Listening to God* Bible reading series, *Daily Guidance* (Cumberland House), the *Amazing Book of Bible Facts* (Marshall Pickering), *Crash Course in Christian Teaching* (Hodder & Stoughton), *Dictionary of the Bible* (co-author; Macmillan/Cumberland House), *Bible Stories* (Parragon), *Common Worship Lectionary* (Oxford University Press), *Handbook of Bible Promises* (co-author; Eagle) and *I Never Knew That was in the Bible* (Nelson).

He and his wife live in Aylesbury and have a son and a daughter.

Stephen Curtis was educated at The Queen's College, Oxford, where he took a first-class degree in Modern Languages, and at the University of York. He was an English lecturer for ten years and, after a brief spell as a Co-op milkman and call-centre interviewer, joined the publishing firm of Collier Macmillan as a lexicographer in 1984. Since 1988 he has worked as a freelance lexicographer, translator and writer. He has recently contributed to, among others, the Encarta *World English Dictionary*, *The New Penguin English Dictionary* and Chambers' *Dictionary of World History*. He is author of *Increase Your Word Power* and (also with Martin Manser) *The Wordsworth Crossword Companion*. He lives in Bath.

PENGUIN POCKET
WRITER'S HANDBOOK

Martin Manser
Stephen Curtis

PENGUIN BOOKS

PENGUIN BOOKS

Penguin Books Ltd, 80 Strand, London WC2R 0RL, England
Penguin Group (USA) Inc., 375 Hudson Street, New York, New York 10014, USA
Penguin Group (Canada), 90 Eglinton Avenue East, Suite 700, Toronto, Ontario, Canada M4P 2Y3
(a division of Pearson Penguin Canada Inc.)
Penguin Ireland, 25 St Stephen's Green, Dublin 2, Ireland
(a division of Penguin Books Ltd)
Penguin Group (Australia), 250 Camberwell Road, Camberwell, Victoria 3124, Australia
(a division of Pearson Australia Group Pty Ltd)
Penguin Books India Pvt Ltd, 11 Community Centre, Panchsheel Park, New Delhi – 110 017, India
Penguin Group (NZ), cnr Airborne and Rosedale Roads, Albany, Auckland 1310, New Zealand
(a division of Pearson New Zealand Ltd)
Penguin Books (South Africa) (Pty) Ltd, 24 Sturdee Avenue, Rosebank, Johannesburg 2196, South Africa

Penguin Books Ltd, Registered Offices: 80 Strand, London WC2R 0RL, England

www.penguin.com

First published as *The Penguin Writer's Manual* 2002
This abridged version first published 2006
1

Copyright © Penguin Books, 2002, 2006
All rights reserved

The moral right of the authors has been asserted

Set in 8.25/12 pt PostScript ITC Stone Serif
Typeset by Rowland Phototypesetting Ltd, Bury St Edmunds, Suffolk
Printed in England by Clays Ltd, St Ives plc

Contents

Acknowledgments   vi

Introduction   vii

1   Grammar   1
2   Usage   65
3   Spelling   152
4   Punctuation   163

Glossary of grammatical terms   202

Acknowledgments

The writers acknowledge with gratitude Nigel Wilcockson's comments on drafts of the text and Robert Allen's advice on points of usage in chapter 2.

Introduction

The *Penguin Pocket Writer's Handbook* is intended as a guide and companion for anyone who wants to write or is faced with the task of writing.

It helps you to learn how to write good and correct English by presenting in a clear and easily understandable way the rules, both written and unwritten, that underpin communication in English. It contains sections on grammar, usage, spelling, and punctuation.

There is no great secret to being a writer. There is no universal 'open sesame' that suddenly makes everything clear for everyone. That is, perhaps, bad news. The good news is that with care, common sense, and practice, everyone should be able to write plainly and well, or learn to write better and more confidently. Even if there is no universal key, it is still the authors' hope that every reader will find in this book guidance and encouragement to turn writing into a rewarding activity.

Martin Manser
Stephen Curtis

I Grammar

Introduction

In Tom Stoppard's play *Travesties*, there is a scene in which the Dadaist poet Tristan Tzara takes a copy of Shakespeare's sonnet 'Shall I compare thee to a summer's day?', cuts it up into individual words with a pair of scissors, puts the words into a hat, and proceeds to draw them out again one at a time at random to create a new 'poem'.

If there were such a thing as a language without grammar, it would be rather like the words in that hat – a jumble, a meaningless collection – and the process of communicating in that language would be as haphazard as the Dadaist method of creating poetry. In fact, all languages have a grammar, and all users of language must know something of the grammar of the language they are using in order to be able to communicate in it at all. Children, unknowingly, learn grammar as they learn to speak and as they gradually increase the range and sophistication of the things they are able to say. They quickly learn the difference between a statement (*I want some*), a question (*Can I have some?*), and a command (*Give me some*) – three types of utterance to which grammar books might devote whole chapters. People frequently complain that they do not know any grammar or were never taught any grammar, but only the second of these complaints is likely to be strictly true.

The point is, of course, that knowledge exists at different levels. Most people nowadays know what a computer is. They can describe what a computer looks like from the outside and roughly what it can do. They can probably use one. Only an expert, though, can describe what a computer is like on the inside and precisely how it functions. The average user of language is perhaps like the average computer user – getting along quite happily until something goes wrong, at which point everything suddenly becomes technical and incomprehensible and someone with specialist knowledge is needed to put matters right.

The purpose of the book is to give ordinary users of English some of the technical know-how they need to solve language difficulties if they should arise. It is also intended to help them acquire some inside knowledge of the way the English language actually works. Last but not least, it may also help them to become more able and confident communicators in a medium that is one of the most versatile and expressive methods of conveying thoughts and feelings that has ever existed.

Types of grammar

Languages are continually evolving. This is most obvious in the additions to vocabulary that are needed to cope with technological advances and other alterations to the landscape of everyday life. Words come into use and fall out of use again. Computers, for instance, have spawned an enormous number of new words, some of which have already fallen into disuse as the technical processes they refer to have become outmoded. The way existing words are used changes too – to take one obvious example, the word *gay* whose main meaning nowadays is 'homosexual' rather than the centuries-old meaning of 'cheerful' or 'bright'.

Grammar also evolves – but usually at a much slower pace because it is largely presented in the form of rules and for everyone who wants to change a rule there are usually others who want to preserve it. From time to time, however, attempts are made to overhaul the way in which we describe the grammatical structure of languages completely. One such attempt was made in the mid-twentieth century by the US linguist Noam Chomsky and his followers. While Chomsky's work has had a profound effect on the academic study of linguistics, most ordinary discussion of language is still conducted on the basis of more traditional concepts and rules. For the purposes of this book, therefore, grammar means traditional grammar.

Technical terms

There are a number of technical terms that the non-technical reader has to be familiar with in order to be able to understand fully what a grammar book or even an ordinary dictionary is trying to say. Most of the basic concepts of grammar are explained and illustrated as they are discussed in the following pages. There is also a brief glossary of terms at the end of the book. Someone who has no previous knowledge of language terminology may, however, find the following brief list useful for understanding its opening sections. A **noun** is a word that stands for a thing, a person, or quality (*book*, *reader*, and *readability* are all nouns). A **pronoun** is a short general word that can replace a noun. A **personal pronoun** is a word such as *I*, *you*, *her*, or *them*. A **verb** is a word that stands for an action (*be*, *have*, *kick*, and *spend* are all verbs). An **adjective** is a word that provides more specific information about a noun (*happy*, *hot*, *red*, and *terrible* are all adjectives). An **adverb** is a word that provides more specific information about a verb or an adjective (*happily*, *terribly*, and *very* are all adverbs). A word that is **singular** refers to one person or thing only, one that is **plural** refers to two or more. *Child* and *adult* are singular nouns; *children* and *adults* are plural nouns. *Is* is a singular form of the verb to be; *are* (as in *we are* or *they are*) is a plural form.

Sentences

As soon as words are taken and used to communicate meaning, they form **sentences**. It is usually assumed that any sentence must contain a verb, but it is better, perhaps, to start from the principle that a sentence is a unit of language that makes sense and is complete in itself. The normal convention for writing a sentence is that it should begin with a capital letter and end with a full stop, a question mark, or an exclamation mark. Under certain circumstances a single word could satisfy all these requirements:

> *No.*
>
> *Really?*
>
> *Impossible!*

Such single-word communications, along with slightly longer phrases such as:

> *For sale.*
>
> *No parking.*
>
> *Once bitten twice shy.*

are known grammatically as **minor sentences** – *minor* because they contain no verb.

Major sentences are sentences that contain a verb. They too can be very short but still meaningful and complete in themselves:

> *Listen!*
>
> *I see.*
>
> *Is that so?*

More often, however, major sentences contain other material – for example, a subject, a verb, an object, or words or phrases modifying any of these – and consist of more than one clause.

Clauses

A **clause** is, like a sentence, a meaningful series of words. Unlike a sentence, however, a clause is not always complete in itself as regards the meaning that it conveys or the action that it describes. Compare the two statements *I arrived late* and *Although I arrived late*. The first simply states a fact; there is not necessarily anything more to be said. The addition of *although* (or any similar word such as *when* or *because*) has the effect of implying that there must be more to say about the incident. In that sense, it is not complete in itself.

A clause that is complete in itself is known as a **main clause**. Every major sentence must have at least one main clause, and a main clause on its own can constitute a satisfactory sentence. A clause that is incomplete in itself is known as a **subordinate clause**.

A sentence may consist of a main clause on its own: *I ran all the way*. It may consist of two or more linked main clauses: *I ran all the way | and arrived completely out of breath*. It may consist of a main clause together with one or more subordinate clauses: *I ran all the way because I was afraid of being late*. (For more on these, see pp. 17–26.)

The parts of a clause or sentence

All clauses or sentences apart from the most simple ones are made up of different parts. These parts, which may consist of a single word or a group of words, are known as the subject, the verb, the object, the complement, and the adverbial. They are discussed individually in the sections below.

The subject

The **subject**, as its name suggests, is what the sentence is about, often the person or thing that carries out the action of the verb in the clause or sentence. In the sentences *Jane called a taxi* and *Money isn't everything*, the subjects are *Jane* and *Money*. To take a more complex example, in the sentence *Drinking wine with lunch makes me feel sleepy in the afternoon* the subject is *Drinking wine with lunch*. The subject can also be a subordinate clause (*How you do it doesn't really matter* in which the subject is *How you do it*) or consist of two or more nouns or pronouns (*Robert and I are very alike in that* in which the subject is *Robert and I*).

The usual position of the subject is at the beginning of the sentence in front of the verb, as in all the examples above. The subject, however, changes its position in certain types of sentence. In questions the subject normally follows the verb:

Are you there?

How did the dog get out?

It may also be placed after the verb following a piece of direct speech (*'There's going to be trouble,' said Anne*), for emphasis (*Out went the lights*), or in clauses introduced by words such as *hardly* or *no sooner* (*No sooner had I left than the guests arrived*).

Whatever its position in the sentence, the subject determines the form of the verb. If the subject is singular, the verb must be singular; if the subject is plural, the verb must be plural: *The rose is red* but *Roses are red*. The same rule applies if the subject is replaced at the beginning of the sentence by *there*: *There is a fault in the software* (*is* because *fault* is singular); *There have been problems with the photocopier* (*have* because *problems* is plural).

The verb

The characteristics and functions of verbs will be discussed more fully in a later section (pp. 48–59) of this book. Suffice it to say at this point that the **verb** is often the focus of a sentence, conveying the most important information in it, as in the following sentences:

He spat at me!

It really hurt.

The verb may simply act as a bridge between the subject and the other components of the sentence that relate to it. This is especially the case with so-called **linking verbs** such as *to be* and *to seem*. In sentences such as *The man in the brown overcoat smoking a cigar is a distant relative of the Duke of Loamshire*, the important pieces of information come before and after the verb (*is*): *The man in the brown overcoat smoking a cigar* and *a distant relative of the Duke of Loamshire*. The verb itself is little more than a convenient way of getting from the one to the other.

The object

The **object** of a sentence is a word denoting a person or thing affected by the action of the verb. There are two possible types of object in a sentence: a direct object and an indirect object. The **direct object** is the person or thing directly affected by the action of a verb. In the sentence *The car hit a tree*, the direct object is *a tree*. In the more complex sentence that was used to illustrate the subject *Drinking wine with lunch makes me feel sleepy in the afternoon* the direct object is *me*. It is usually possible to ascertain which word is the direct object of a sentence by asking a question about it beginning with *what?* or *whom (who?)*: *What did the car hit?* – a tree. *Whom does drinking wine make sleepy?* – me. Like the subject, the object can also be a subordinate clause (*They explained why the television keeps breaking down*) or consist of two or more nouns or pronouns (*She took Celia, Jane, and me to the cinema*).

An **indirect object** is an additional object that occurs with some verbs, especially verbs that involve the action of giving. In the sentences *He gave me a kiss* and *They bought their daughter a flat in London*, the direct objects are *a kiss* and *a flat in London* respectively. The indirect objects are *me* and *their daughter*. The question that uncovers the indirect object is *to whom?* or *to what?* or *for whom?* or *for what?* For example, *What did they buy?* – a flat (direct object). *For whom did they buy it?* – their daughter (indirect object). Indirect objects are usually used together with direct objects, not on their own.

The usual position of both the direct and indirect object in the sentence is after the verb. If there are two objects the indirect object (highlighted here by underlining) is almost always placed before the direct object:

> *Give me the gun.*
>
> *She told the man what was happening.*

If both the direct and the indirect object are pronouns (*me*, *him*, *her*, *it*, etc.), the direct object (highlighted) is sometimes placed first, especially in informal speech:

> *Give it me.*
>
> *I sent it them weeks ago.*

The complement

In sentences where the verb is a linking verb of the type mentioned briefly above (*to be*, *to seem*, *to feel*, etc.), what follows the verb is not an object but a **complement**. In the sentence *James is a computer expert*, the complement is *a computer expert*. A complement, in simple terms, is a word or group of words that tells us more about the element of the sentence that it relates to. In the example just given, the phrase *a computer expert* is a subject complement because it contains a description of the subject of the sentence *James*. A subject complement usually follows the verb and takes the form of a noun or an adjective or a noun or adjective phrase, as in: *The task seemed utterly impossible* and *She became a fully paid-up member of the union*.

The adverbial

The **adverbial** is the part of the sentence that provides more information about the verb and the action it denotes. It may consist of a single word, an adverb, as in the sentence *They chose the site carefully* – where the adverbial is *carefully*. It may, however, consist of a phrase or a subordinate clause. In the following sentences:

> *I'm leaving first thing tomorrow.*
>
> *Put the book on the shelf.*
>
> *The picnic was cancelled because it was raining.*

the adverbials are, respectively, *first thing tomorrow*, *on the shelf*, and *because it was raining*. There may also be more than one adverbial in a sentence: *I'm leaving | first thing tomorrow | on a plane to Singapore.*

The adverbial is usually positioned after the verb at the end of the sentence, as in all the above examples. It may also, however, be placed at the beginning of the sentence or between the subject and the verb.

> *With trembling hands she opened the package.*
>
> *I immediately left the room.*

Agreement of verbs

As explained in the section on the subject (pp. 6–7), the form of the verb is decided by the nature of the subject. The correspondence that must exist between subject and verb is an example of what is known in grammar as **agreement** or **concord**. For a sentence to function as a satisfactory whole, there must be agreement between its component parts.

Since verbs in English generally have the same form in a particular tense whether the subject is singular or plural, agreement between verb and subject is not as great a problem in English as it is in some other languages. It does, however, sometimes cause difficulty in verbs such as *to be* or *to have* that change their form more frequently than other verbs. Rules of agreement make the phrases *you was* or *he do* incorrect – the form of the verb does not agree with the pronoun: the correct standard forms are *you were* and *he does*.

Agreement also dictates the form of subject and object complements. If a subject or object is plural, its complement must be plural as well: *Jan is an executor* but *She made Jan and Gordon executors of her will*. Agreement also determines which form of the **reflexive pronoun** (*myself*, *yourselves*, etc.) or the **possessive** (*my*, *your*, etc.) should be used. This usually involves little difficulty, but it is obviously important to distinguish between *You can please yourself* (addressed to one person) and *You can please yourselves* (addressed to more than one).

Troublesome grammatical point:
agreement of verbs 'Neither Jean nor her sister is coming' or
'Neither Jean nor her sister are coming'

Though keeping to the rules of agreement in English is usually a simple matter, there are occasions when it is difficult to determine whether the subject is singular or plural. When the subject consists of two nouns joined by *and* there is no problem, because the subject is obviously plural:

Jean and her sister are coming.

Both Jean and her sister are members.

But where the subject consists of two nouns linked together with *either . . . or* or *neither . . . nor*, the situation is less clear. If both or all of the nouns involved are singular, then the verb should be singular: *Neither Jean nor her sister (nor her mother) is coming.* If the nouns involved are all plural, the verb should be plural: *Either the Wilkinsons or the Petersons have the key.* Where one of the nouns is singular and the other plural, the usual rule is that the verb agrees with whichever stands nearest to it:

Neither Jean nor her brother and sister know (rather than *knows*) *anything about this.*

Either those curtains or that carpet has (rather than *have*) *to go!*

The same applies if two different personal pronouns figure in the sentence: *Neither he nor I have* (rather than *has*) *done anything we ought to be ashamed of.* (A little rewriting can often avoid any problems or awkwardness that might arise when trying to apply the rule of agreement in such cases.)

A similar difficulty may arise when the subject takes the form of a singular noun linked to a plural by *of*: *a number of things*; *a collection of paintings*; *a procession of visitors*. It often seems more natural to put the verb into the plural form. Although *a number* is strictly a singular form, few people would insist on replacing the plural *have* with the singular *has* in the sentence *A number of things have cropped up.* In other instances, however, standard English offers a choice, depending on whether the speaker wishes to emphasize the unity of the group or the multiplicity of the things or people that make it up: *His collection of paintings is going to be sold* (considered as a unity) in contrast to *A collection of miscellaneous objects were being sold off as a job lot* (considered as a multiplicity). (See also pp. 29–30.)

Types of sentence

Sentences fall into four main categories: statements, questions, directives (i.e. commands, instructions, or requests), and exclamations.

Statements

The commonest type of sentence is a **statement**. It begins with a capital letter, ends with a full stop and presents the listener or reader with a piece of information without necessarily expecting any response from them. *My husband took the dog for a walk along the towpath* is a statement, and it has its components in the standard order – subject followed by verb, followed by object, followed by adverbial.

Questions

Questions – which end, of course, with a question mark instead of a full stop – ask for information instead of presenting it and usually expect a response from someone. The distinguishing mark of the majority of questions is a reversal of the normal word order of sentences and the placing of the verb before the subject. The statement *He is busy* is turned into a question by the reversal of the first two words: *Is he busy?* The order of subject and verb is similarly reversed following a question word such as *how*, *when*, *where*, *why*, etc.:

>*How did I know?*

>*Why didn't you tell me?*

It is not, however, always necessary to reverse the subject and verb. The way that a person speaks a sequence of words in the normal order can turn it into a question – the pitch of the speaker's voice usually rises towards the end of what he or she is saying. Instead of saying *Would you like some tea?*, it is possible to say *You'd like some tea?* with the pitch of the voice rising towards the end of the sentence with the same effect. The variation in the pitch of the speaker's voice is called **intonation**.

There are also questions known as **tag questions**. These are statements with a little tag such as *isn't it?*, *aren't you?*, or *won't they?* tacked on the end:

>*He's messed it up again, <u>hasn't he</u>?*

>*It isn't time to go yet, <u>is it</u>?*

Notice that the tag usually reuses the main verb or part of it (*He's* (he has) . . . *hasn't he*; *isn't* . . . *is it*). If the main verb is not, or does not contain, *be*, *do*, *have*, or *will*, etc., *do* is used to make a tag:

>*He smokes, doesn't he?*

>*She drove here, didn't she?*

Notice also that a positive main clause takes a negative tag and vice versa:

>*He's happy today, isn't he?*

> *He's not happy, is he?*

On the use of question marks, see pp. 178–9.

Directives

Directives are orders or requests to other people to do or to stop doing something. They usually have no subject because it is obvious from the situation who is being addressed. The verb is in what is known as the **imperative**, the command form, which is identical with its base form (see pp. 57–9):

> *Stop!*
>
> *Listen!*
>
> *Sit down, shut up, and eat your breakfast!*

Orders such as these end with an exclamation mark.

Not all directives are so abrupt. Instructions, invitations, and requests also use the imperative form of the verb:

> *Bake in a moderate oven for 20 minutes.*
>
> *Come to lunch with us next Sunday.*
>
> *Please pass the butter.*

The negative form of the imperative in ordinary English is made using *do*:

> *Don't say that!*
>
> *Do not exceed the stated dose.*

The straightforward negative form of the imperative is usually found only in older literary works: *Judge not that ye be not judged*

(The Bible, Matthew 7:1, Authorized (King James) Version). *Do* can also be used to add emphasis to an instruction or request (*Oh, do stop talking and get on with it*) or warmth to an invitation (*Do come, we'd love to see you*). For the sake of politeness, directives are often rephrased as questions, especially using *would* or *could*:

> *Would you open the door for me, please?*
>
> *Could you not smoke in here?*

Exclamations

Exclamations – which always end with an exclamation mark – express a person's spontaneous reaction to a situation, usually one of surprise, approval, or annoyance. They often take the form of a minor sentence without a verb:

> *What fun!*
>
> *More power to your elbow!*

Longer exclamations sometimes follow the normal word order of statements *It's a girl!* Many exclamations, however, begin with *how* or *what* and in these the object or complement is placed before the subject and the verb:

> *How strange it seems!*
>
> *What a wonderful time we all had!*

On the use of exclamation marks, see pp. 180–81.

Interjections

Interjections are a group of words that have the exclamatory function of expressing an emotion such as surprise, approval, anger, or pain: *ah!*, *oh!*, *mmm!*, *ouch!*, *ugh!*, *psst!* They are more commonly used in spoken English; in written English they are rarely used except in direct speech.

Sentence structure

A simple sentence, that is a simple major sentence, consists of a single clause. As mentioned above (p. 5), a main clause on its own can constitute a satisfactory sentence: *The sun is shining today*. A sentence with more than one clause is known as a **multiple sentence**. Multiple sentences may consist of more than one main clause or a main clause together with a number of **subordinate clauses**. Again, as mentioned earlier (p. 5), a subordinate clause is one that is not complete in itself and cannot, on its own, form a satisfactory sentence. Subordinate clauses usually begin with words such as *that*, *which*, *if*, or *when*.

Compound sentences

A multiple sentence consisting of two or more main clauses is called a **compound sentence**. Compound sentences are linked together by *and*, *but*, *or*, *yet*, or *while*:

> *Henry is a lorry driver and Jane works part-time in a supermarket.*
>
> *We do stock those boots, but we haven't any in your size.*

Generally speaking the order of the clauses can be reversed without affecting the sense of the sentence: *Jane works part-time in a supermarket and Henry is a lorry driver*. The process of linking clauses or other parts of a sentence together in this way is known as **coordination** (see pp. 19–20). The above examples all illustrate simple coordination between two clauses, but multiple co-ordination is also possible: *The band was still playing and everyone was still dancing, but, for me, everything had suddenly changed*.

Troublesome grammatical point:
using 'and' or 'but' at the beginning of a sentence

The main function of *and* and *but*, which are known as **coordinating conjunctions**, is to link items within sentences. It is often suggested that it is either bad grammar or bad style to begin a sentence with either of them. Neither suggestion is correct. While it is inadvisable to use them to open a sentence too often, they can be used very effectively in the right circumstances: *But, soft! what light from yonder window breaks? It is the east, and Juliet is the sun . . .*

Complex sentences

A multiple sentence consisting of a main clause and one or more subordinate clauses is called a **complex sentence**. The subordinate clause usually follows the main clause:

> *They went for a walk, | while we tidied up the house.*
>
> *I can't come | because I'll be in London on Tuesday.*

The subordinate clause may also, however, begin the sentence: *Since you're busy, I'll call again later.*

Coordination

Coordination is the grammatical process of linking together elements of a sentence that have equal status. The section on 'Compound sentences' (pp. 17–18) considers how it operates with clauses in compound sentences. It also operates between individual words or phrases:

> *Do you take milk and sugar?*

> *The day was fine but rather chilly.*

> *You could drive over the bridge or through the tunnel.*

These are all examples of **linked coordination** – i.e. a linking word *and*, *or*, or *but* is used in all of them. It is, however, possible to coordinate words, phrases, or clauses by using punctuation marks instead of the linking words, in which case the process is known as **unlinked coordination**. Instead of saying *It was a cold and frosty morning* it is perfectly possible to say *It was a cold, frosty morning*. Likewise, the *but* in the sentence *James likes coffee, but Henry prefers tea* could be replaced by a semicolon: *James likes coffee; Henry prefers tea*.

It should be noted that when two nouns or noun phrases are linked by *and*, two different combinations can be produced. Compare the sentences, *Jane and Joe kissed the bride* and *Jane and Joe kissed*. The former sentence could be split into two clauses: *Jane kissed the bride and Joe kissed the bride*. The technical name for combining two noun phrases in this way is **segregatory coordination**. The second sentence, *Jane and Joe kissed*, cannot be split in the same way and still make sense. The two terms form a unit, as they do, for example, in the sentences *Management and* *unions met yesterday* and *Oil and water don't mix*. The technical term for this is **combinatory coordination**.

Subordinate clauses

The grammatical name for the relationship between parts of a sentence that do not have equal status is **subordination**. The parts of the sentence that show subordination are the incomplete or subordinate clauses (see pp. 5–6 and p. 17).

Subordinate clauses can perform many functions. They can substitute for any part of the sentence except the verb, appearing, for instance, as the subject: *How it got there is a mystery*, as the direct or indirect object:

> *She doesn't know what's going on.*
>
> *I'll give a prize to whoever comes up with a workable solution.*

or as the adverbial: *It broke while I was trying to clean it*. It is also possible to use a subordinate clause as a part of, or as an addition to, one of the main elements of the sentence, for example, after a noun as part of the subject or object:

> *The book that you lent me was very useful.*
>
> *I haven't finished reading the book that you lent me.*

All the examples of subordinate clauses shown so far have contained a **finite** verb (that is a verb in the present, past, or future tense; see p. 52). These are called **finite clauses**. It is also possible for subordinate clauses to be based on an **infinitive** (the root form of the verb, such as *(to) be* or *(to) carry*, see pp. 52–4), or a **participle** (a form of the verb ending in *-ing* (present participle) or *-ed*, etc. (past participle), see pp. 54–6). In the sentences *They* *were happy to see us again* and *I was just walking along, minding my own business*, the phrases *to see us again* and *minding my own business* are **non-finite clauses**.

Comparative clauses

A **comparative clause** is a special type of subordinate clause that expresses a comparison between two or more things. There are two kinds of comparisons: those in which the two things being compared are equivalents and those in which they are not.

Equivalence is shown by using the construction *as . . . as*:

> *She is as clever as you are.*

> *I waited as long as I could.*

Note that, for grammatical purposes, the relationship is one of equivalence even in a sentence such as: *She is nowhere near as clever as you are.* Non-equivalence is shown by a combination of a **comparative element**, either an adjective ending in *-er* (*bigger*, *smaller*) or a phrase containing a word such as *more* or *less*, and a clause that begins with *than*:

> *She's a lot taller than I am.*

> *He's doing less well now than he was a year ago.*

In both types of sentence it is usual to drop any parts of the subordinate clause that repeat what is in the main clause:

> *She is as clever as you (are).*

> *He's doing less well now than (he was) a year ago.*

> *The job took far less time than (we) expected (it to take).*

Comment clauses

Comment clauses are short clauses inserted into a sentence to show the speaker's attitude to what he or she is saying or to make clear what he or she is trying to do. Phrases such as *I'm glad to say*, *I'm sorry to say*, *to be frank*, or *to put it another way* are typical examples. Unlike other types of clause, they do not relate to a particular component of the sentence, but to the sentence as a whole, and, for that reason, can be inserted in it at almost any point:

> *To be honest, it doesn't make much difference.*
>
> *It doesn't make much difference, to be honest.*
>
> *It doesn't, to be honest, make much difference.*

Comment clauses are more often used in spoken than in written English and are quite frequently used simply, as it were, to fill a gap. This is especially the case with phrases such as *you know*, *you see*, or *I mean*: *Well, I mean, it's a tricky situation.*

Reporting what someone has said

There are two ways of conveying what someone has said. It is, of course, possible to write down the exact words that the person used in inverted commas: *'I'm sorry, but I can't help you,' she said.* This is known as **direct speech**.

There are two parts to a sentence containing direct speech: the **reporting clause**, consisting of a subject and a verb of saying (in the above example *she said*), and the **reported clause**, the words spoken: *I'm sorry, but I can't help you*. The reported clause is the part in inverted commas.

The reporting clause can also be placed before, after, or in the middle of the reported clause. If it is placed after or in the middle, the normal order of subject and verb is often reversed: *'It looks very black outside,' said Jill* (or *Jill said*), *'I think it's going to rain.'* Note that subject and verb are not usually put in reverse order when the subject is a personal pronoun: *'Come on,' he said, 'let's go'* – not *said he* because it sounds old-fashioned and definitely not *shouted he, called he,* or *answered he.*

Reported or **indirect speech** is a method of conveying what someone said without using inverted commas. It integrates the speaker's words into the framework of a sentence. This is usually done with a clause beginning with *that*, although the actual word *that* is often omitted: *She said (that) she was sorry, but (that) she couldn't help us.* In some cases a *wh-* word (*what, where,* etc.) appears: *They asked us where we had been.*

There are a number of adjustments that have to be made when direct speech is changed into reported speech. The personal pronoun in the reported clause has to be changed: *She said, 'I'm sorry'* becomes *She said she was sorry.* Often changes need to be made to references to time or place: *They said, 'It'll be ready next week'* might, for instance, have to become *They said last week that it would be ready this week.* *If* or *whether* usually needs to be inserted when transferring a question: *'Can we come too?' they asked* becomes *They asked whether* (or *if*) *they could come too.* Notice also that the reporting clause always come before the reported clause in indirect speech, no matter where it is placed in direct speech.

The most significant change, however, is in the tense of the verb in the reported clause (see p. 49). The present tense in the reported clause of direct speech becomes the past tense in indirect speech: *'I'm coming,' he said* becomes *He said he was coming.*

The future tense formed with *will* becomes the future-in-the-past formed with *would*: *'I will be there,' she said* becomes *She said she would be there*. The simple past tense or the past tense formed with *have* becomes the pluperfect tense formed with *had*: *'We've finished,' they announced* becomes *They announced that they had finished*.

Relative clauses

Relative clauses are clauses that begin with words such as *that*, *which*, *who*, *whose*, etc., which are known as **relative pronouns**, or the words *when* and *where*, which are known as **relative adverbs**. The main function of relative clauses is to give more specific information about the nouns they follow, as in *the boy who brought the message* or *the book that I lent you* or *a place where we can be alone*.

There are two types of relative clause and it is often important to be able to distinguish between them. The first type is called a **restrictive** or **defining clause** – the information that such a clause contains is intended to identify a particular person or thing specifically as the one that is being talked about. The second type is called a **non-restrictive** or **non-defining clause**. The information that it contains is incidental, an extra. The clause could be omitted from the sentence in which it appears without making it unclear who or what is being referred to.

The difference between these two kinds of relative clause can be seen in the two following examples:

The paragraph that mentions you by name comes about
halfway down the page.

The paragraph, which comes about halfway down the page,
mentions you by name.

In the first example the crucial piece of information (the fact that
someone is mentioned by name) is put into the relative clause *that*
mentions you by name. This clause defines which paragraph is being
talked about. In the second example the crucial information is in
the main clause and the fact that the paragraph is halfway down
the page is put in as a useful but optional extra. That is the nature
of a non-restrictive relative clause.

The same form of words can often be used or interpreted either
restrictively or non-restrictively. For example, consider the sentence *My uncle who lives in Nottingham is a retired headmaster*.
If someone were discussing all their uncles, then this might be
read as a restrictive clause *My uncle who lives in Nottingham is a*
retired headmaster, and my uncle who lives in Derby is a grocer, and as
for my uncle who lives in Leicester, he's a milkman. Uncle by uncle
they are being specifically identified by the towns in which they
live. On the other hand, perhaps the conversation is not about
uncles but about teaching. In this case the fact that the speaker's
uncle lives in Nottingham is really neither here nor there: *My*
uncle, who lives in Nottingham, is a retired headmaster, and what he
thinks is . . .

Non-restrictive clauses are usually enclosed in commas or dashes
to indicate that they are dispensable from the sentence: *Paulton –*
which is where I grew up – is a small village in Somerset. It is incorrect
to put commas or dashes around a restrictive clause: *The paragraph*
that mentions you by name comes about halfway down the page.

When a non-restrictive relative clause refers to a thing, it must begin with the relative pronoun *which*:

> *The car, which was at least forty years old, rattled alarmingly.*
>
> *Paulton – which is where I grew up – is a small village in Somerset.*

Restrictive clauses relating to things may begin with either *that* or *which*, although there is an increasing tendency for *that* to be preferred: *The card that/which I eventually chose was a humorous one.* If, as in the last example, the noun that the relative pronoun (*that*, *which*, or *whom*) relates to is the object of a restrictive clause, then the relative pronoun can be omitted: *The card I eventually chose was a humorous one.*

On the use of commas in non-restrictive clauses, see also pp. 171–3.

One further type of relative clause should be mentioned – it is called a **sentential relative clause** because it relates not to a specific word but to a whole clause or to the whole of the rest of the sentence. Such clauses are also introduced by *which*: *He was late for his appointment – which was not like him at all.*

Word classes: nouns

The following sections of this survey of grammar deal with individual types or classes of words, their nature and functions, and the changes that they undergo when they are used for different purposes. A **noun** stands for a person or thing. The word 'thing', in this instance, is being used in its widest sense, because nouns denote not only real-world objects or creatures (*table* is a noun, as are *bus*, *computer*, *lion*, and *virus*), but also events and actions and completely intangible things such as states, feelings, and concepts (*business* is a noun, as are *conversation*, *inertia*, *happiness*, and *unity*).

Types of noun

Nouns are usually classified by type – although many of them belong, or can belong, to more than one type – and these types are usually dealt with in contrasting pairs. There are proper nouns and common nouns, concrete nouns and abstract nouns, countable nouns and uncountable nouns, and collective nouns. These types will now be dealt with individually.

Proper nouns and common nouns

A **proper noun** is a noun that denotes a specific person or thing. It is, to all intents and purposes, a name. In fact, **proper name** is an alternative term for proper noun.

Proper nouns include people's first names and surnames, the names of places, times, events, and institutions, and the titles of books, films, etc. They are spelt with an initial capital letter: *Sam*, *Shakespeare*, *New York*, *October*, *Christmas*, *Christianity*, *Marxism*, and *Coronation Street*.

All nouns that are not proper nouns are known as **common nouns**. The same word can be both a common noun and, in other contexts, a proper noun. An *enigma* (common noun) is a mystery, for example; *Enigma* (proper noun) is the name of a German encoding machine used in the Second World War, the title of a novel, and the name the British composer Edward Elgar gave to the theme on which he based his *Enigma Variations*. *Road* is a common noun when used in the sentence *I was walking down the road* and part of a proper noun in the name *London Road*.

Apart from being spelt with an initial capital letter, proper nouns have other characteristics that usually distinguish them from common nouns. They do not, generally, have a plural and they are not, usually, preceded by *a* or *an*. There is only one *Australia*; there was only one *Genghis Khan*.

Although this is the general rule, however, there are many exceptions to it. There are occasions when either a specific example or several examples of something denoted by a proper noun must be referred to: *keeping up with the Joneses*; *buying a Picasso*; *one of the warmest Januaries on record*.

Proper nouns are quite often preceded by *the*: *the United Nations*, *the White House*, *the Olympic Games*. The *t* of *the* is spelt with a capital letter only when it forms an integral part of the name or title: *a copy of 'The Times'*; *a conference held at The Hague*.

Concrete nouns and abstract nouns

Concrete nouns stand for actual objects that can be seen, touched, tasted, etc. **Abstract nouns**, as the name implies, denote things that are abstract and cannot be seen or touched. *Table* and *lion* are concrete nouns; *happiness* and *unity* are abstract nouns. Many nouns have both concrete and abstract senses, the abstract sense often being a figurative or metaphorical version of the concrete one. Thus *key* is a concrete noun when it means an object that unlocks a door, an abstract one in a phrase such as *the key to the problem*.

Countable nouns and uncountable nouns

Countable nouns are nouns that can form a plural and can be preceded by *a* or *an*: *a table – tables*; *an equivalent – equivalents*. Countable nouns must, in fact, be preceded by a *determiner* (a word such as *a*, *the*, *this*, *that*, or *my*; see p. 41) when they are singular. It is not possible, for example, to say *table stands*. Concrete nouns tend to be countable – though by no means all are.

Uncountable nouns are nouns that do not normally form a plural and cannot normally be preceded by *a* or *an*. They can, however, stand alone without a determiner (see p. 42) when they are singular. Concrete uncountable nouns include words such as *blood*, *mud*, and *foliage*; *concrete* in its normal everyday sense of a building material is an uncountable noun. Abstract nouns tend to be uncountable – words such as *happiness*, *gravity*, or *inspiration*.

There are many words that have both countable and uncountable senses. *Tea*, for example, is uncountable in phrases such as *a packet of tea*, *a cup of tea*, or *invite someone for tea*. Three different senses are involved and in each of them *tea* is uncountable. In the phrase *two teas please* (= cups of tea) it is, however, countable. *Feeling, emotion,* and many similar words are uncountable when they are used generally and abstractly (*Try to put more feeling into the way you say the line*) and countable when they refer to specific types or examples (*a feeling of joy; One can only guess at what their feelings were on that occasion*).

Collective nouns

Collective nouns are nouns that refer to a group of people or things. *Group* itself is a collective noun, as are *committee, crew, government, flock, herd, team,* etc.

Troublesome grammatical point:
using a singular or plural verb with a collective noun 'The
government is united' or 'The government are united'

Most collective nouns are countable; their peculiarity is that when
they are used in the singular form they can take either a plural or
a singular verb. It is possible to say that *the government is united* or
the government are united. It is possible to say *the team has lost its
last five matches* or *the team have lost their last five matches*. Choosing
a singular verb treats the group as a unit; choosing a plural one
emphasizes the fact that it is made up of many individuals. While
it may be difficult sometimes to decide whether to opt for a singular or plural verb, it is very important that all the attendant words,
such as possessive pronouns, match the form that has been chosen
for the verb – so it would be incorrect to write either *the team has
lost their last five matches* or *the team have lost its last five matches*.

The plural of nouns

Most English nouns form their plural by adding *-s*: *table – tables*;
team – teams. Nouns whose singular form ends in *-ch*, *-s*, *-sh*, *-ss*,
-x, or *-zz* add *-es* to make the plural: *bunch – bunches*; *cross – crosses*.
Nouns that end in one or more consonants and *-y* (*lady*, *shanty*,
monarchy, etc.) change the *y* to *ie* and add *s* in the plural (*ladies*,
shanties, *monarchies*) (see p. 155). All these plural forms are **regular**
– that is to say that they follow the standard pattern for a particular
feature or operation in a language.

Many common English words have **irregular** plurals – in other
words they do not conform to the standard pattern. Obvious
examples are words such as *man* and *woman* (plurals *men* and
women) or *mouse*, *child*, and *foot* (plurals *mice*, *children*, and *feet*

respectively). It is partly because these are very basic, common words with a long history in the English language that they have retained these unusual plurals, which were, in fact, regular in the forms of the language that were the ancestors of modern English.

Words that end in the letters *-f* (or *-fe*) and *-o* frequently cause difficulty because some of them have regular plurals and some have irregular ones. The plural of *thief* is *thieves*, but the plural of *chief* is *chiefs*. *Life* pluralizes as *lives*, but *fife* as *fifes*. Eminent people have been caught out by the fact that *potato* and *tomato* become *potatoes* and *tomatoes*, although large numbers of words ending *-o* simply add *-s* (*avocados*, *pianos*, *photos*, and *radios*). See also pp. 155–6.

There are no easy rules, unfortunately, for irregular plurals in English. They simply have to be learnt and remembered.

Foreign plurals

There are a number of words that have been imported into English directly from foreign languages and have retained a foreign form as their only plural or, increasingly nowadays, as an alternative to a regular English one. The majority of these come from Latin or Greek. The more specialized and technical they are, the more likely it is that they will retain a Latin or Greek plural.

Latin nouns usually end in *-a*, *-ex* (or *-ix*), *-um*, or *-us*. The Latin plural of *-a* is *-ae*, while that of *-us* is *-i*, and words whose singular form ends in *-um* have a plural ending *-a*. *Larva* and *vertebra* become *larvae* and *vertebrae* in the plural, *nucleus* and *stimulus* become *nuclei* and *stimuli*, *bacterium* and *stratum* become *bacteria* and *strata*.

Words taken from Greek that have irregular plurals tend to end in *-is* or *-on*. Words whose singular form ends in *-is* usually end in *-es* in the plural (*basis* – *bases*; *crisis* – *crises*). Words such as *criterion* and *phenomenon* have plurals that end in *-a* (*criteria* and *phenomena*).

It should be noted that the fact that a word ends in one of the above combinations of letters does not automatically mean that its plural will be one of the irregular ones mentioned above. It is quite correct to speak of *arenas* or *eras*, *foetuses*, *sinuses*, *albums*, *museums*, *complexes*, *coupons*, and *electrons*. In fact to foist a Latin or Greek plural on any of these words would be incorrect. Additionally, there are quite a number of words where a more learned Latin or Greek plural exists side by side with an ordinary English one: *formulas* is as correct as *formulae*, *mediums* as correct as *media*. Sometimes one sense of a word usually has a Latin or Greek plural and another sense an English one. *Medium* is a case in point: communicators with the dead are *mediums*, means of mass communication are *media*.

Among the plural forms taken from modern foreign languages, perhaps the most noteworthy are words from French ending in *-eau*, which can form their plural as *-eaux* or *-eaus* (*bureaux* or *bureaus*, *tableaux* or *tableaus*), and words from Italian ending in *-o*, whose plurals can end in *-s* or *-i* (*tempos* or *tempi*, *virtuosos* or *virtuosi*).

This is an area of English usage where changes are currently taking place. On the whole, irregular forms from foreign languages are tending to be used less and ordinary English forms more. Though dictionaries do not always agree, a modern dictionary is the best place to look for guidance both for the spelling of tricky English plurals (*-os* or *-oes*) and to ascertain whether a foreign or an English form is more appropriate.

Zero plurals and invariable nouns

Nouns that change their form in the plural, whatever form that change may take, are known as **variable nouns**. Nouns that do not change their form are either zero plurals or invariable nouns.

A **zero plural** is a noun whose form does not change whether it is singular or plural. The word *sheep*, for example, remains the same whether a single animal or a flock is being referred to. A single *aircraft* in the sky or a dozen *aircraft* at an airfield may be described. There are a number of nouns, especially names of animals, which are sometimes treated as standard nouns and sometimes as zero plurals. The plural of *fish* is sometimes *fish* and sometimes *fishes*. There are *elephants* at the zoo or in a circus, but on the plains of Africa (that is to say, when using the word in a slightly more technical, zoological way) you are more likely to report seeing *elephant*.

Invariable nouns are nouns that are either always singular or always plural. The commonest type of invariable singular noun is the uncountable type (e.g. *mud* or *gravity*) discussed on p. 29. In addition, there are a number of nouns ending, rather confusingly, in *-s* which are strictly singular: *billiards*, *mumps*, *news*. None of these should be followed by a plural verb:

> *News has* (not *have*) *just come in . . .*

> *Mumps is* (not *are*) *a serious disease.*

Many of the words ending in *-ics* fall into this category, although many of them also have senses in which they can be used with a plural verb: *Politics is the art of the possible*, but *His politics* (= his political views) *are very right wing*.

Among the nouns that are invariably plural there are some that look plural because they end in *-s* (*dregs*, *glasses* (= spectacles), *scissors*, and *trousers*) and some that do not look as if they are plurals (*cattle* and *vermin*). They are always, however, followed by a plural verb:

> *My trousers are at the cleaners'.*
>
> *The cattle are grazing in the field.*

The gender of nouns

English does not divide nouns into masculine and feminine, or masculine, feminine, and neuter as ancient languages did and many foreign languages still do. English nouns show gender only in as much as they relate either to males or to females: *woman* is not a feminine word in the grammatical sense that *la femme* is in French or *die Frau* is in German, but it, obviously, refers to a female human being as *boy* refers to a male one. There are many similar pairs of words that describe animals of different sexes (*cock* and *hen*, *ram* and *ewe*, etc.), but these words too are not either masculine or feminine in the grammatical sense. Gender in this sense is most important, for grammatical purposes, in that it determines the form of the personal pronoun which is used in connection with a noun. Female creatures are referred to as *she*, *her*, males as *he*, *him*, and inanimate objects (and occasionally very young children) by the non-personal *it*.

There are a number of suffixes (word endings) that can be used to convert a noun that usually refers to a male into one that refers to a female. The commonest of these is *-ess*. A female lion is a *lioness*, the daughter of a king or queen is a *princess* and a woman actor may be referred to as an *actress*. Though it is not a grammatical issue as such, it is worth noting that the use in jobs and positions of gender-specific terms, especially women-only terms, is declining. This is an area where changes are currently taking place in the language in response to changes in society. It is usually inappropriate to employ a gender-specific term where a neutral one is available, and so -*ess* (and -*ette* and -*trix*) words should generally be avoided.

The possessive form of nouns

In many languages, nouns have different inflections depending on their role in the sentence, for example, whether they are the subject or object of a verb. An inflected form of a noun is known as a **case**. English nouns remain in their basic form – in what is known as the **common case** – except where it is necessary to show that one person or thing owns another. There is a **possessive** or **genitive case** for most English nouns. In the singular, it consists of adding apostrophe *s* to the base form: *Jill's car; a climber's equipment; the car's service history*. This rule applies also to singular nouns that end in -*s* (*Robert Burns's poetry; the dress's sleeves*). Plural nouns that end in -*s* add an apostrophe only: *members' voting rights; the animals' feeding time*. Plural nouns that end in a letter other than *s* add an apostrophe *s* as usual: *the children's toys; the media's obsession with smut*. (See also pp. 198– 200.)

An alternative way of showing possession – the more frequent way for inanimate objects – is to use *of*: *the top of the hill; the history of the United States*.

Nouns as modifiers

A feature of modern English is its use of nouns as **modifiers** – words which provide more information about other words and describe the things or people that they stand for more specifically. Nouns are frequently used in front of other nouns in the way that adjectives are. In the phrases *car keys* and *house keys*, *car* and *house* are modifiers. Many everyday nouns are very frequently used in this way as a neater alternative to a longer phrase using, for example, the genitive with *of*, so that *the roof of the church* becomes *the church roof* and *the window of the kitchen* becomes *the kitchen window*.

Nouns used as modifiers may look like adjectives, but they do not share all their characteristics. They cannot be used in any position except in front of the noun they relate to and they do not have *comparative* or *superlative* forms (see pp. 39–40).

Noun phrases

A **noun phrase** is a group of related words, one of which is a noun or pronoun. It may consist simply of a single noun or pronoun, a noun preceded by *a* or *the*, or a main noun accompanied by a phrase or clause. The following are all noun phrases based on the main noun *child*: *a child*; *a small child*; *a child with learning difficulties*; *a child who is of above average intelligence*.

Apposition

When a noun phrase is immediately followed by another noun phrase that refers to exactly the same person or thing and defines him, her, or it more closely, the two phrases are said to be in **apposition** to each other. For example, the following noun phrases are in apposition: *Paris, the capital of France*. Strictly speaking, the order in which the two phrases in apposition appear should make no difference to the meaning of the sentence:

> *Paris, the capital of France.*
>
> *The capital of France, Paris.*
>
> *Dr Brown, the head of the French department, is giving the lecture.*
>
> *The head of the French department, Dr Brown, is giving the lecture.*

Similarly, it should be possible to omit either of the two elements without making the sentence incomprehensible:

> *Dr Brown is giving the lecture.*
>
> *The head of the French department is giving the lecture.*

The term *apposition* is also, however, more loosely applied to cases where the two phrases cannot be transposed so freely (*my computer, a Gateway 2000* but not *a Gateway 2000, my computer*), where a word or phrase such as *namely* or *for example* comes between the two phrases in apposition (*her favourite poets, namely Keats and Shelley*), or where the second element cannot be dropped if the sense is to be preserved: *The play* Under Milk Wood *is on the radio tonight*. If the title of the play were omitted, the sense would be much less clear.

Appositive clauses

Appositive clauses are clauses beginning with *that* which are attached to abstract nouns such as *belief, fact, knowledge, suggestion*, and which indicate their content, that is, what is believed, known, suggested, or a fact: *the belief that God exists*; *the fact that she is away on holiday*. They are called appositive because their relationship to their main noun is the same as that between one noun phrase and another in apposition to it: Paris *is* the capital of France; the fact in question *is* that she is away on holiday.

It is important to distinguish between appositive clauses beginning with *that* and restrictive clauses beginning with *that* (see pp. 24–6) – for example between *the idea that was put forward at the meeting* and *the idea that the meeting should be postponed*. The first clause is a relative clause – *that* could be replaced by *which* and does not convey the content of the idea – the second is an appositive one.

Adjectives: types

Adjectives are words that describe particular qualities possessed by people or things. They are usually attached to or relate to nouns. Words such as *big*, *new*, *old*, *red*, and *small* are adjectives.

They are defined in two ways: according to their position in relation to the noun they relate to and according to whether or not they can form comparisons.

An **attributive adjective** is one that appears before the noun it relates to, as in *a red dress* or *bright colours*, where *red* and *bright* are adjectives used attributively. Some adjectives can be used only in this position, for example, *former*, *latter*, or *utter*.

A **predicative adjective** is one that is used after a verb such as *be*, *become*, or *seem* – in other words, it is the complement of its noun. In the sentences *The dress is red* and *The colours seem very bright*, *red* and *bright* are being used predicatively. Some adjectives can be used only in this position, for example, *afraid*, *asleep*, or *alike*.

Occasionally an adjective is placed immediately after the noun it relates to, in which case it is said to be **postpositive**. Postpositive adjectives are most often found together with pronouns, as in:

There's something fishy going on.

Everything possible is being done.

Here *fishy* and *possible* are being used postpositively. But there
are a number of fixed noun phrases that contain a postpositive
adjective (*body politic*, *court martial*, *princess royal*), and when the
past participles of verbs (see p. 55) are used as adjectives, they often
occur postpositively (*the money invested*, *the people involved*, *the time
required*).

Gradable and non-gradable adjectives

Most adjectives are **gradable**, that is to say that they stand for a
quality which can vary in degree. In other words, it is sensible to
ask *how . . . is something?* and expect an answer *very, slightly, totally,*
or *more . . . than something else*. Gradable adjectives can be used in
comparisons or can be modified by adverbs such as *very, completely,
fairly, slightly*. There are a number of adjectives, however, that,
because of their sense, are **non-gradable**. To ask *how perfect, how
impossible,* or *how unique* something is does not make sense –
or does not, strictly speaking, make sense. Those adjectives are
therefore non-gradable.

Comparative and superlative

The **comparative** form of an adjective is, as its name suggests,
the form used when making comparisons. Shorter and simpler
adjectives in English form the comparative by adding *-er* (*lighter,
sweeter*). Adjectives that end with a single vowel followed by a
single consonant (*big, red*) double the consonant (*bigger, redder*)
(see pp. 158–9). Adjectives that end in *-y* change to *i* (*angrier, warier*)

(see p. 155), although single-syllable adjectives may sometimes keep the *-y* (*drier* or *dryer*). Adjectives that end in *-e* simply add *-r* (*bluer, later*). Longer adjectives – those with three syllables or more – form their comparatives with *more* (*more comfortable*; *more unusual*). Most adjectives with two syllables can form the comparative either way (*commoner/more common*; *shakier/more shaky*).

The comparative form should be used when comparing people or things in twos or when comparing one person or thing with another. This is the case even if an individual is being compared with a group or with a series of individuals:

> *This is the <u>cheaper</u> of the two options.*

> *John is <u>taller</u> than his brother or his father.*

> *Mary is <u>more troublesome</u> than all the rest of the children put together.*

The form used to indicate that a thing possesses a quality to a greater degree than two or more other things is the **superlative**. The superlative is formed in the same way as the comparative either by adding *-est* or by using *most* (*sweetest*; *biggest*; *driest*; *commonest/most common*; *most comfortable*). At least three things must be involved in a comparison for the superlative to be the appropriate form of the adjective to use – though it is also used when the number of things involved is unspecified:

> *John is the <u>tallest</u> of the three boys.*

> *It is the <u>cheapest</u> option currently on offer.*

The order of adjectives

Adjectives are often used in strings of two or more before nouns and are sometimes separated by commas. When they are used in this way, certain conventions usually dictate the order in which they appear. It is not idiomatic, for instance, to write *a red Italian fast car* or *a country remote village*. The usual order of adjectives (sometimes changed for emphasis or special effect) is first general adjectives (*big, fast, remote*), followed by parts of verbs used as adjectives (*excited, thrilling*), followed by adjectives of colour, followed by adjectives of nationality or region (*Chinese, Italian, Western*), followed by nouns used as adjectives or adjectives closely derived from nouns (*country, iron, wooden*). Reordered on these principles, the phrases shown above would reappear as *a fast red Italian car* and *a remote country village*.

Determiners

Determiners are a small but very important class of words that, like adjectives, appear in front of and relate to nouns. They include *a, the, this, that, all, each, every, few, more, much, many, some, which, whichever*, and *what*. Their function is to determine or specify the particular object or person, or the number of objects or persons, in a group that a noun refers to. Numerals (*one, two, three*, etc., and *first, second, third*, etc.) are also classed as determiners, as are also the possessive adjectives *my, his, her, your*, etc.

The position of determiners

Determiners, unlike most adjectives, must come before the noun they relate to – but they are also frequently used as pronouns. As is not uncommon in language, the same word can play different roles in different contexts. In the phrases *all the people* and *some green apples*, *all* and *some* are determiners; in the sentences *All is not lost* and *Save some for me*, *all* and *some* are pronouns. *All* and *some* also count as pronouns when followed by *of* in phrases such as *all of the time* or *some of the people*.

A noun may be preceded by more than one determiner (*each and every day*; *my one hope*; *all the many tributes*) or by a determiner and one or more adjectives (*a few happy days*; *more long sleepless nights*).

Determiners and nouns

Determiners are often limited as to the type of noun that they can accompany. The following determiners can be used only with singular countable nouns – *a*, *an*, *each*, *either*, *every*, *neither*, and *one* (*a book*, *each book*, etc.). The following are restricted to use with plural countable nouns *both*, *few* (and *a few*), *many*, *several*, *these*, *those*, together with *two* and all the other numerals (*both books*, *a few books*, etc.). Finally, *least*, *less*, *little* (and *a little*), and *much* are only used with uncountable nouns (*less applause*, *much applause*).

The articles

The commonest determiners are *a* and *the*, known respectively as the **indefinite article** and **definite article**. *A* is known as the indefinite article because, in a phrase such as *a book*, any book could be meant, whereas *the book* must refer to a book that has been referred to at least once before and is defined or definite to that extent.

Pronouns

Pronouns are words that can take the place of nouns and noun phrases, and sometimes of clauses. They are stand-in words, but vitally important for avoiding long-winded repetition. Consider for instance the unlikely passage:

> *James picked up the book. James carried the book over to James's sister Jenny and showed Jenny a passage. 'Isn't the passage in the book interesting?' James asked.*

If the pronouns *he*, *it*, *his*, *her*, and *this* are put in appropriate places instead of the names and nouns, it immediately becomes more readable:

> *James picked up the book. He carried it over to his sister Jenny and showed her a passage. 'Isn't this interesting?' he asked.*

Personal pronouns

The most important class of pronouns contains the **personal pronouns**, words such as *I*, *you*, *he*, *she*, and *it* which stand for the names of the people and things that are the actual actors in sentences.

Personal pronouns are divided first of all according to **person**. For grammatical purposes, there are three persons. The **first person** is the speaker – if singular *I*, if plural *we*. The **second person** is the person spoken to – in both singular and plural *you*. The **third person** is the person (or object) spoken about by the first and second persons – in the singular, according to gender, *he*, *she*, or *it*, and in the plural always *they*.

The forms of the personal pronouns illustrated so far are those for the **subject case**, the forms used when the pronoun is the subject of the sentence. When a pronoun is the object of the sentence and when it follows a preposition, it goes into the **object case**: *I* becomes *me*; *we* becomes *us*; *he*, *she*, and *they* change to *him*, *her*, and *them* respectively; and *you* and *it* remain the same:

> *I ran.*
>
> *He ran me over.*
>
> *They shouted.*
>
> *She shouted at them.*

Troublesome grammatical point:
the pronoun after a preposition 'Between you and I' or 'Between you and me'

In ordinary English grammar, prepositions are followed by the object form of the personal pronoun – that is to say the form that would be used as the object of a simple sentence (*me, you, him, her, it, us, them*). So *He hit me*, therefore *behind me* and *Give it to me* – not *behind I*, etc. (*I* is a subject form). *Between* is a preposition just the same as *behind*, or *to*, and follows the same rule: *We divided the inheritance between us* (not *between we*). It makes no difference to this rule how many pronouns follow the preposition. Consequently, the correct form is *between you and me* (just as it would be *behind us* and *them* or *to both him and her*).

Possessive pronouns

The personal pronouns also each have their own distinctive possessive forms. We have already touched on the forms that are used

as determiners: *my, your, his, her, its, our,* and *their.* The forms that
are used as pronouns are: *mine, yours, his, hers, its, ours,* and *theirs.*
These forms can be used as either the subject or complement of a
verb:

> *That bag is mine.*
>
> *Yours is over there.*

It should be noted that although most of the forms of the possessive pronoun end in *s,* none of them ends in an apostrophe *-'s.*

Reflexive pronouns

The **reflexive pronouns** are a small group of words formed by
adding *-self* (singular) or *-selves* (plural) to either the objective or
the possessive forms of the personal pronoun: *myself, yourself,
himself, herself, itself, ourselves, yourselves,* and *themselves.* They are
used to show that the action of a verb affects the person or thing
that is its subject – effectively that the same person or thing is
both the subject and the object of the verb:

> *She fell down and hurt herself.*
>
> *The machines switched themselves off.*

Sometimes they follow a preposition rather than the actual verb,
but still refer back to the subject: *He looks very pleased with himself.*

Emphatic pronouns

Emphatic pronouns are exactly the same in form as reflexive
pronouns (*myself, himself,* etc.). They usually follow immediately

after the noun or pronoun they relate to and, as their name suggests, their function is purely to give emphasis:

> *I myself have said as much on numerous occasions.*

> *It's not the fault of the machine itself, but of the person operating the machine.*

Sometimes the emphatic pronoun is moved to a position further away from the word it relates to, but its function remains the same: *He didn't actually say so himself, but his best friend told me that that's what he feels.*

Demonstrative pronouns

The **demonstrative pronouns** are *this*, *that*, *these*, and *those* when used as pronouns rather than determiners. They are called *demonstrative* because they point out or demonstrate which of a number of things are being referred to. *This* (singular) and *these* (plural) usually refer to things nearer to the speaker, *that* (singular) and *those* (plural) to things further away:

> *Whose book is this on my desk?*

> *Whose car is that parked on the other side of the road?*

> *Take these and put them over there with those.*

Interrogative pronouns

Interrogative pronouns begin questions. There are five of them: *who*, *whom*, *whose*, *what*, and *which*. (Other words that begin questions, such as *how*, *when*, and *where*, are called **interrogative**

adverbs.) *What* and *which* can be used before any type of noun, singular or plural:

> *What size do you take?*
>
> *Which shoes are you taking?*

Who, whom, and *whose* are effectively three different forms of the same word. *Who* is a subject pronoun. *Who was at the meeting?* or in a reported question *I asked her who was at the meeting. Whom* is an object pronoun:

> *Whom should we ask?*
>
> *She told me whom she had spoken to.*

Note that in modern English, especially modern spoken and informal English, *whom*, though grammatically correct, would generally be replaced in both these examples by *who*.

Whose is the possessive form: *Whose are these trainers?*

On the use of question marks, see pp. 178–9.

Relative pronouns

A **relative pronoun** is the word *that, which, who, whom,* or *whose* when used to begin a **relative clause** (see pp. 24–6). *Which* is always used to refer to animals or things; *who* and *whom* are always used to refer to people. *That* usually refers to things, but sometimes to people; *whose* usually refers to people, but sometimes to things.

Indefinite pronouns

Indefinite pronouns are pronouns that refer to people or things without stating specifically who or what they are. Indefinite pronouns such as *anyone*, *everybody*, *nobody*, or *somebody* are used to refer to people only; the corresponding forms, such as *anything*, *everything*, *nothing*, and *something*, refer only to things. Other indefinite pronouns such as *all*, *both*, *some*, etc., may refer to either people or things.

Verbs: their forms

Verbs are a large, very important, and rather complex class of words. They denote action, in its broadest sense. Words such as *go*, *talk*, and *walk* are verbs. A verb is the one essential component of a major sentence.

Most English verbs have four or five forms. Regular English verbs, that is verbs that conform to the basic standard pattern for verbs, have four. The verb *cook*, for example, has a base form *cook*; a form ending in *-s*: *cooks*; a form ending in *-ing*: *cooking*; and a form ending in *-ed*: *cooked*.

The base form is used to make the **infinitive** form (p. 52) *to cook*, the **imperative** form (see pp. 15–16; used for giving orders – *ready*, *steady*, *cook!*), and all the forms of the present tense except the third person singular (*I cook*, *they cook*, etc.).

The only function of the *-s* form is to make the third person singular of the present tense (*he cooks*, *she cooks*, *it cooks*). Note that just as nouns ending in *-ch*, *-ss*, etc., add *-es* to make their plural, verbs ending in the same combination of letters also add *-es* (*teaches*, *kisses*, *mixes*), verbs that end in *-y* change it to an *i* and add *-es* (*glorifies*, *tries*) (see p. 155), and that verbs ending in *-o* usually add *-es* (*echoes*, *embargoes*) (see pp. 155–6).

The *-ing* form of the verb makes the present participle (see p. 54) (*cooking*) and the *-ed* form makes both the past tense (*we cooked*) and the past participle (see p. 55) (*cooked*).

Irregular verbs usually have one additional form – a past participle that is different from the past tense: *sing, sings, singing, sang* (past tense), and *sung* (past participle). Both the past tense and the past participle are completely different from the *-ed* forms of regular verbs. Nevertheless, the various parts of irregular verbs serve the same function as those of regular verbs.

The tenses of verbs

The **tenses** of verbs are the different time frames within which the action of the verb takes place. The *present tense* refers to action taking place now (*I cook; we are cooking*). The *past* and *future tenses*, obviously enough, refer to action in the past or future (*I cooked; she has cooked; they will cook*).

It will be noticed that the four or five forms of the verb discussed above provide only two of the tenses – the simple present (*you cook; he cooks*) and the simple past (*we cooked*). In order to make all the other tenses, another verb is used: *be, have*, or *will*. These are known as **auxiliary verbs** (see p. 51). Using auxiliary verbs it is possible to fill the time gaps left by the main forms of the verb.

Continuous tenses

Continuous tenses express actions that are going on, were going on, or will be going on at a particular time. They are constructed using *to be* together with the *-ing* form of the verb. The continuous present tense (*I am cooking*) is in fact commoner in everyday use than the simple present tense. *He cooks* often means *he is able to cook*, whereas to express the idea that he is at this time standing by the stove holding a frying pan, you would say *he is cooking* – he is doing it now. The same distinction holds for past time, where the past continuous tense is used especially to refer to an action that was going on when something else occurred: *She rang while I was cooking the lunch*.

The future tense

The **future tense** in English is usually formed using the auxiliaries *will* or *shall*. A distinction used to be drawn, especially in British English, between the first person *I* and *we*, which were strictly supposed to make their future tense with *shall* (*I shall cook tomorrow* or in the continuous form *we shall be cooking tomorrow*), and the second and third persons (*you* and *he, she, it*, and *they*), which made their future tense with *will*. To say *I will* (as in the marriage service) or *you shall* or *they shall* expressed a special determination to do something or to see something done (*Britons never, never, never shall be slaves!*). For the most part, however, this distinction is less strictly observed than it once was. The future tense is commonly formed nowadays with *will* (often informally shortened to -*'ll*) for all persons of the verb.

Perfect tenses

The **perfect tense** of a verb is a past tense formed with the auxiliary verb *have* together with the -*ed* form of a regular verb or the past participle of an irregular verb (*I have cooked; I had sung*).

When formed with the present tense of *have*, the perfect tense replaces the simple past tense in questions (*Have you told him?*), when emphasizing that a thing has been done (*Yes, I have told him*), or to indicate that an action that began in the past is still continuing in the present (*He has left the key at home and has gone back to get it*).

When formed with the past tense of *have*, the perfect (also called the *pluperfect* here) expresses an action that occurred at an earlier time than the past time of the main action:

> *I had been there before, so I knew what to expect.*

> *After he had locked up the building, he went home.*

Auxiliary verbs

Auxiliary verbs are verbs that are used with and in front of other verbs. Besides *be*, *have*, *will*, and *shall*, the auxiliaries that have already been mentioned while discussing tenses, there is the verb *do*, which is used to make variant and slightly more emphatic forms of both the present and the past tense:

> *I do sometimes make mistakes.*

> *She did say she was coming.*

They are also used to form questions in both those tenses:

> *Do you cook?*

> *Did you see that?*

The other auxiliaries express ability (*can*, *could*), obligation (*must*, *should*), wishes (*would*), or possibility (*may*, *might*). All the auxiliaries except *be* and *have* are always followed by the base form of the verb:

> *I can cook.*

> *You must sing for us.*

> *They might come.*

Finite and non-finite verbs

A **finite** verb is any verb that has a specific tense, is in one of the three persons, and is either singular or plural. Generally speaking, a finite verb is a verb that has a subject (even if that subject is not expressed, as, for example, in the **imperative** or command form of the verb). A **non-finite** verb does not fit this description. The non-finite forms of the verb are the infinitive (the base form usually preceded by *to*: *to sing*), the present participle (*singing*), and the past participle (*sung*).

The infinitive

The **infinitive** with *to* is used after many verbs, nouns, and adjectives:

> *He learnt to sing in a church choir.*
>
> *I've no wish to sing.*
>
> *She's too nervous to sing for us.*

It can also form the subject of a verb (*To sing refreshes the soul*) or express a purpose like *in order to* (*To sing you don't have to be able to read music*).

The infinitive without *to* is only used after other verbs, especially auxiliaries:

> *She might sing, if you asked her.*
>
> *I heard Pavarotti sing once.*

Troublesome grammatical point:

splitting an infinitive 'to <u>sweetly</u> sing'

The infinitive of verbs in English is usually written as two words: *to* + the basic unchanged form of the verb: *to do*, *to go*, *to sing*, etc. In Latin and most modern European languages, however, the infinitive is represented by a single word, so that the equivalent of *to sing* in Latin is *canere*, in French *chanter*, in German *singen*, etc. On this basis, some teachers of English grammar argue that, though expressed in two words, the English infinitive is a single unified concept, and that it is bad grammar to insert any other word or phrase between, for example, *to* and *sing*. That is what is meant by 'splitting an infinitive', as in *to usually do*, *to not infrequently go*, or *to sweetly sing*. (Note that only a phrase of this sort counts as a split infinitive – in phrases such as *to be sweetly singing* or *to have usually done*, the adverbs (*sweetly*, *usually*) do not come between the two constituent parts of the infinitive, *to* and *be* and *have* respectively.)

The most famous example of the late twentieth century was '. . . to boldly go where no man has gone before', from the introduction to the television series *Star Trek*.

Some people say that you should never split an infinitive. Most guides to usage, however, advise a common-sense approach. If you can put the adverb before *to* or after the main part of the verb without making the sentence sound awkward or ambiguous, then do so:

> . . . *boldly* to go where no man has gone before.

> . . . to go *boldly* where no man has gone before.

However, moving the adverb sometimes makes the meaning unclear:

They planned to secretly exchange the prisoners.

They planned secretly to exchange the prisoners.

The first sentence contains a split infinitive, *to secretly exchange*. But if you move *secretly* before *to exchange*, as in the second sentence, it is not clear whether the adverb relates to the verb *planned* or *exchange*.

Sometimes a split infinitive simply sounds more natural, especially in informal spoken English:

You're supposed to partly cook the vegetables first.

You need to really thump the keys.

Participles

The **present participle** is used to make the continuous forms of verbs and in some clauses (*before/after/while cooking the dinner . . .*). Present participles are also sometimes used as adjectives (*a singing waiter*) and sometimes as nouns (*Singing lifts the spirits*). When the present participle is used as a noun, it is sometimes preceded by a possessive form (*Does my singing disturb you?*).

Troublesome grammatical point:
pronoun + the '-ing' form 'Do you object to my bringing my sister?' or 'Do you object to me bringing my sister?'

From a grammatical point of view, the choice between *Do you object to my bringing my sister?* and *Do you object to me bringing my sister?* hinges on whether the phrase *bringing my sister* should be considered to be more like a noun or more like a verb. If it is more noun than verb, then the possessive *my* is more appropriate – as it would be in a more straightforward question, such as *Do you object to my comings and goings?*, where *comings* and *goings* are plural nouns. Constructing a different sentence in which the phrase is the subject of a sentence backs up the point – *My bringing my sister might cause problems* sounds far preferable to *Me bringing my sister might cause problems*. This is because it seems wrong for the object form *me* to play a part in the subject of a sentence. The form of the question with *my* is more correct and preferable in standard and formal writing. But in more informal English the form with *me* is common and generally acceptable.

The **past participle** is used to form the perfect tenses of verbs and the **passive** (see p. 57). It is also used as an adjective (*a cooked dinner*; *a sung Mass*) and can form the basis of a clause: *Exhausted by his efforts, he collapsed on the sofa*.

Troublesome grammatical point:
dangling participle 'Blown to bits by the blast, workers were removing rubble from the buildings'

A so-called **dangling participle** is a phrase based on a present or past participle (an '-ing' form or, usually, an '-ed' form) – in this case *blown to bits by the blast* – that is wrongly or ambiguously placed so that it is not clear what or whom it refers to. The result is commonly a howler: *Blown to bits by the blast, workers were removing rubble from the buildings*. It was the buildings, not the workers, that were blown to bits. The safest place for a participle clause is next to the noun it describes (in this instance, the buildings): *Workers were removing rubble from the buildings blown to bits by the blast*. Consider this other example which is a less obvious mistake: *Through the window we saw, flying over the foothills of the Andes, a flock of scarlet parrots*. It could be that we are flying in an aircraft looking out, or that we are on the ground watching flying parrots. It would be clearer if the sentence were rearranged so that *flying over the foothills of the Andes* came next to *we* (*Flying over the foothills of the Andes, we saw through the window . . .*) or *parrots* (*. . . we saw a flock of scarlet parrots flying over the foothills of the Andes*).

Transitive and intransitive verbs

A **transitive** verb is one that has a direct object (*bring* a packed lunch); an **intransitive** verb does not have a direct object (*winter came late that year*). Verbs that describe movement are often wholly or mainly intransitive:

> *Prices are rising.*
>
> *Prices are falling.*
>
> *The army advanced.*
>
> *The army retreated.*

Many verbs can be used both transitively and intransitively: *I can't sing* (intransitive); *She can't sing a note* (transitive). Verbs often come in pairs that have a similar form, one being transitive and the other intransitive. *Rise*, for example, which is always intransitive, has a transitive partner *raise*:

> *Prices are rising again.*
>
> *They have raised their prices again.*

Active and passive

The **active voice** is a form of a verb in which the subject performs the action denoted by the verb: *Hugh cooked the supper*. The **passive voice** is a form of a verb in which the subject is affected by the action of the verb: *The supper was cooked by Hugh*. Another way of expressing this is to say that the object of an active verb (in the above example *the supper*) becomes the subject of a passive verb in an equivalent sentence: *The supper was cooked by Hugh*. The subject of the active sentence (*Hugh*) becomes the passive **agent** in the passive one – usually preceded by the preposition *by*. It follows from this that only transitive verbs can be used in the passive, as an intransitive verb has, by definition, no object to form the subject of a passive sentence. The passive form is constructed using the auxiliary verb *be* together with a past participle: *The song is (being) sung/was sung/will be sung by . . .*

Moods

There are three so-called **moods** of verbs. The **indicative** is the ordinary form of the verb used for making statements or asking questions. The **imperative** (that consists of the base form of the verb on its own without a subject: see pp. 15–16) is used for giving orders. The **subjunctive** is a special form of a verb that is sometimes used in clauses expressing a wish, demand, or recommendation. The present tense of the subjunctive for most verbs is the same as the ordinary present tense, except that the third person singular form drops its final *-s* or *-es*: *lest he forget*; *I suggest she give it more thought*. The present subjective of *to be* is *be* and of *to have*, *have*:

Lest I be thought remiss, I shall inform you immediately.

They insisted he have another try.

Using the subjunctive makes a sentence much more formal and the same result can be obtained with less formality by using *should*. *Should* could be inserted into all the above examples:

Lest I should be thought remiss . . .

I suggest she should give it more thought.

They insisted he should have another try.

The present subjunctive is most often used in certain fixed phrases:

God bless you!

If need be . . .

Suffice it to say . . .

Long live the Queen!

Only the verb *to be* has a separate form for the past tense of the subjunctive, *were* as in *if I were you*. The past subjunctive is preferable to the ordinary past tense after *if* when something completely hypothetical is in question:

Even if that were the case . . .

What would you say if I were to tell you I'd won the lottery?

It is incorrect, however, to use *were* when the speaker is not putting forward a hypothesis but using an *if* clause to introduce a statement of fact or probability:

If she was upset, she certainly didn't show it.

If it was there this morning, it's probably still there now.

Phrasal verbs

Phrasal or **multi-word** verbs are verbs in which the base form is accompanied by an adverb or a preposition or both: *do down; do up; do away with*. These verbs usually have distinct meanings that are not always deducible from their component parts – *do down* means 'to criticize adversely', *do up* means 'to fasten', *do away with* means 'to get rid of'. Grammarians tend to distinguish between true phrasal verbs, which have their own, usually figurative, meaning and combinations of the verb in its literal sense together with a preposition or adverb: *run out of* is a phrasal verb in the sentence *We've run out of milk* but not in the sentence *He ran out of the room*. In most instances the object of such a verb follows the adverb or preposition, as in the examples above. But when a phrasal verb consists of a verb and an adverb the object can usually either follow the adverb or come between it and the verb: *She did up her coat* or *She did her coat up*.

Adverbs

Adverbs are a versatile class of words that can be used to modify words, phrases, or whole sentences. They are used especially often with verbs, adjectives, or other adverbs.

The majority of adverbs derive from adjectives and are formed by adding *-ly* or *-ally* to the base form of the adjective. The adjective *sad* becomes the adverb *sadly*, *original* becomes *originally*, and so on. The meaning of adverbs can often be rendered as 'in a (sad, original, etc.) way'.

Besides indicating the manner in which something was done, adverbs often indicate time (*always*, *now*, *often*, *then*, *today*, and *yesterday* are all adverbs, as well *currently*, *formerly*, *simultaneously*, etc.) and place (*here*, *there*, and *everywhere* are all adverbs, as are words like *around*, *down*, *in*, *out*, and *up*, which can also function as prepositions). Like adjectives, many adverbs also have a **comparative** and a **superlative** (see pp. 39–40): *Jack ran fast, Jill ran faster, and the dog ran fastest of all. Fast* is, however, something of an exception. The majority of adverbs form the comparative and superlative with *more* and *most*:

> *The light was shining more brightly than before.*

> *We are the most poorly paid workers in the whole industry.*

The position of adverbs

Adverbs can usually be placed in almost any position within a clause without materially affecting its meaning:

> *Quickly I gathered my things.*

> *I quickly gathered my things.*

> *I gathered my things quickly.*

The one place where it is normally impossible to put an adverb is between a verb and its direct object: *I gathered quickly my things* is not standard English.

Sometimes, however, changing the position of an adverb crucially affects the meaning. *Only this key fits that lock* and *This key fits that lock only* (or *only fits that lock*) do not mean the same. It is usually best to place the adverb next to the word it relates to. When adverbs modify adjectives or other adverbs, they are always

placed before them, for example with *very*: *a very quick change*;
Things are changing very quickly.

Troublesome grammatical point:
a double negative 'I don't know nothing'

See chapter 2, '**double negative**', p. 89.

Adverbial phrases and clauses

The role of an adverb is often performed by a phrase or clause. An
adverbial phrase may be a group of words based on or around
a main adverb (*as soon as possible*; *strangely enough*; *rather
unusually*), but is also often a phrase based on a preposition (*in a
minute*; *beside the lake*; *owing to circumstances beyond our control*).
Adverbial clauses are introduced by words such as *because*, *if*,
when, *where*, and *while*. All such clauses and phrases are also known
simply as **adverbials**: see p. 10.

Prepositions

Prepositions are a group of words mainly consisting of small
words, but they are some of the most frequently used words in the
English language. They are words that are placed before other
words, especially nouns, phrases, or clauses, to link them into
the sentence. *After*, *at*, *before*, *behind*, *for*, *in*, *of*, and *out* are all
prepositions. In the following examples the preposition *in* is followed first by a noun, then by a pronoun, then by an adverb, and
finally by a clause:

There's nothing in the box.

There's nothing in it.

There's nothing in there.

There's nothing in what she says.

Not all prepositions are single words, however; phrases such as *because of, in spite of,* and *on account of* are prepositions too.

Many words that are prepositions also have other functions. *In,* for example, is both an adverb and a preposition. When it is functioning as a preposition, however, it must be followed by something else in order to complete the sense:

They are in the living room (in as preposition).

They are in (i.e. at home; in as adverb).

Before can function not only as a preposition and an adverb, but also as a conjunction:

I managed to do four hours' work before lunch (preposition).

I've never been here before (adverb).

Before you go, let me show you this photograph (conjunction).

Troublesome grammatical point:
ending a sentence with a preposition

'This is the sort of English up with which I will not put' was Sir Winston Churchill's alleged response to the clumsy English produced by those who go out of their way to avoid ending a sentence with a preposition. Many great writers of the past have broken this 'rule':

> *And do such bitter business as the day/Would quake to look on.* (William Shakespeare)
>
> *What a fine conformity would it starch us all into.* (John Milton)
>
> *The present argument is the most abstracted that ever I engaged in.* (Jonathan Swift)
>
> *. . . the less convincing on account of the party it came from.* (Edmund Burke)
>
> *. . . too horrible to be trifled with.* (Rudyard Kipling)

Supporters of the so-called 'rule' that a sentence should never end with a preposition insist that a *pre*position should always *pre*cede its complement. But this is sometimes undesirable or impossible:

> *He gave me some photographs to look at.*
>
> *This seat is not very comfortable to sit in.*
>
> *She had forgotten which page she was up to.*
>
> *This pen is not easy to write with.*
>
> *Was it worth waiting for?*

You would not say *He gave me some photographs at which to look.* Nor would you say *She had forgotten up to which page she was.*

Similarly, the question *Was it worth waiting for?* cannot be expressed in any other way.

However, in formal written English, you can often keep the

preposition before its complement without sounding stilted. You could write *one of the women with whom I work* in a formal letter, for example, though you would say *one of the women I work with* when talking to a friend.

You can also sometimes rephrase a sentence to move the preposition from the end:

> *This pen is easy to write <u>with</u>.* → *It is easy to write <u>with</u> this pen.*

> *This seat is not very comfortable to sit <u>in</u>.* → *Sitting <u>in</u> this seat is not very comfortable.*

Conjunctions

A **conjunction** is a word that links two clauses or two other parts of a sentence. There are two types of conjunction: coordinating conjunctions and subordinating conjunctions.

Coordinating conjunctions link words, phrases, or clauses that have equal status. Examples are *and*, *or*, and *but*, together with the paired joining phrases *both . . . and, either . . . or, neither . . . nor,* and *not only . . . but also*. See also pp. 19–20.

Subordinating conjunctions link parts of a sentence that do not have equal status. Their main function is to introduce subordinate clauses used as adverbials:

> *I only found out <u>after</u> she had left the company.*

> *<u>As</u> you're not a member, you can't vote.*

See also pp. 20–21.

2 Usage

Usage is concerned with words whose use sometimes causes special difficulty or controversy. Although there is inevitably some degree of overlap between grammar and usage, usage is not primarily concerned with the general rules of grammar. Grammar lays down rules, but not everything that it is theoretically correct to say or write according to the rules of grammar is actually good English. Just as judgments handed down by actual courts modify the interpretation of statutes, the usage of language in practice sometimes differs from what its grammar might lead you to expect. So usage stands in a similar relation to grammar as case law does to statute law.

This chapter consists of a series of short entries dealing with words that are often a source of difficulty to users of English. The expressions are listed in alphabetical order.

a or **an**? The rule is that *an* should be used instead of *a* in front of all words beginning with a vowel sound. These include all words whose first letter is *a* or *i*, most words beginning with *e*, *o*, and *u*, and a few beginning with *h*: *an ace*; *an interesting evening*; *an obviously impossible task*. The exceptions among words spelt with an initial vowel are as follows. When *u* is pronounced *yoo*, it is preceded by *a*: *a unit*; *a useful tool*. Words beginning with *eu* (also pronounced *yoo*) take *a*: *a eucalyptus tree*; *a European*. *One* and words beginning with the same sound take *a*: *a one-off*; *a once mighty empire*. Words spelt with an initial *h* that is not pronounced take *an*: *an hour*; *an honour*. It is also not strictly incorrect to write *an hotel* or *an heroic achievement*, and in speaking it may seem less awkward to say *an (h)otel* than *a hotel*. Most modern authorities, however, recommend that words beginning with *h* should be preceded by *a*: *a hacker*, *a horse*, *a historian*, *a hotel*.

Letters of the alphabet and abbreviations made up of letters take *a* or *an* depending on their pronunciation. *B*, *C*, *D*, *G*, *J*, *K*, *P*, *Q*, *T*, *U*, *V*, *W*, *Y*, and *Z* are preceded by *a*: *a BA*; *a V-reg car*. *A*, *E*, *F*, *H*, *I*, *L*, *M*, *N*, *O*, *R*, *S*, and *X* follow *an*: *an MA*; *You form the plural by adding an 's'*.

Aboriginal or **Aborigine**? The indigenous people of Australia are referred to as *Aboriginals* or as *Aborigines* in many dictionaries. This has been replaced, in Aboriginal circles at least, by *Aboriginal* as both noun and adjective.

Aborigine or **Aboriginal**? See **Aboriginal** or **Aborigine**?

about, **around**, or **round**? See **around**, **round**, or **about**?

abrogate or **arrogate**? These two formal verbs are sometimes confused. To *abrogate* something such as a treaty or a right is to 'annul' or 'abolish' it. To *arrogate* is to 'claim or seize something without justification' – it is related to *arrogant* and usually occurs in the form *arrogate something to oneself*: *She has recently arrogated to herself the role of decision-maker for the whole group.*

abuse or **misuse**? There is a subtle distinction between these two words, which are generally similar in meaning both as nouns and as verbs. *Abuse* usually suggests morally improper treatment, often involving a breach of trust: *to abuse someone's hospitality; child abuse. Misuse,* on the other hand, may refer simply to incorrect use (*to misuse a word*), though often with suggestions of moral disapproval as well: *a misuse of taxpayers' money.* Somebody who, for instance, is said to be *abusing* the word 'integrity', may be using it hypocritically or in order to mislead. Somebody who is *misusing* it could be either using it in the wrong meaning or using it inappropriately. Note also that unlike *abuse, misuse* does not normally refer to the treatment of people.

accommodation *Accommodation* is often misspelt. It has two *c*'s, two *m*'s, and two *o*'s.

AD and **BC** *AD* is traditionally written before a number signifying a year: *AD 1625.* This is because the abbreviation *AD* means *anno domini* (in the year of our Lord), and if the phrase were written or spoken in full it would make better sense before the date than after it. This practice is by no means universally adhered to with year numbers, however, and when referring to centuries it is necessary to place *AD* at the end of the phrase: *in the third century AD. BC* always follows a date: *440 BC; the seventh century BC.* In printed text these abbreviations are often written in small capitals: AD and BC.

adverse or **averse**? These two words are sometimes confused. *Adverse* means 'acting against' or 'unfavourable' and is almost always used before a noun: *adverse criticism; adverse weather conditions. Averse* means 'strongly opposed to or disliking', usually comes after a verb, and is followed by the preposition *to: I wouldn't be averse to giving it another try.*

advice or **advise**? The noun *advice* is spelt with a *c*: *a piece of* *advice; Take my advice, don't do it. Advise*, the verb, is spelt with an *s*: *I'd strongly advise you not to do it.*

advise or **advice**? See **advice** or **advise**?

affect or **effect**? These two words, which are pronounced the same, are sometimes confused. *Affect* is a verb that means 'influence or change': *How will this affect my pension prospects? Effect* is most commonly used as a noun: *What effect will this have on my pension prospects?* The rule to remember is: the verb is spelt with an *a*; the noun is spelt with an *e*. *Effect* can also be used, slightly formally, as a verb. In this case its meaning is to 'bring about' or to 'carry out': *The police effected an entry into the premises; Frederick here! O joy, o rapture! Summon your men and effect their capture!* (W. S. Gilbert, *The Pirates of Penzance*).

agenda Although *agenda* was originally a plural noun, it is now always treated as a singular and has its own plural *agendas*: *draw up an agenda; Today's agenda includes a discussion of the financial subcommittee's report.* There is a singular form *agendum* ('an item to be dealt with'), but it is very rare and is best replaced with *item on the agenda.*

aggravate, **aggravation** *Aggravate* is related etymologically to the word *grave* ('serious'). Its oldest surviving meaning is 'to make worse or more serious': *We ought not to do anything that might aggravate the situation.* Some traditionalists contend that this is its only true meaning and disapprove of the use of *aggravate* to mean 'annoy'. This other meaning has, however, been well established for centuries. The use of the noun *aggravation* (often shortened to *aggro*) to mean 'trouble', however, is slang and to be avoided in serious writing.

ain't *Ain't* has never been fully accepted in standard English, though it was commonly used in place of *am not* in the eighteenth century. It is still unacceptable in speaking or writing standard English. See also **aren't**.

all right or **alright**? See **alright** or **all right**?

alright or **all right**? The spelling *alright*, although fairly common, is still considered by many users of English, especially the traditionalists, to be a wrong spelling of *all right*. There is no logical reason why the spelling *alright* should not catch on as the spellings *already* and *altogether* did some centuries ago, to distinguish in writing between *they're all right* (each one is correct) and *they're all right* (they're not bad, they're unharmed). But it has not caught on yet.

alternate or **alternative**? In British English there is a clear distinction between these two words: *alternate* is an adjective and a verb, *alternative* is an adjective and a noun. *Alternate* means 'every other' (*Meetings take place on alternate Wednesdays*) or 'occurring by turns' (*alternate layers of stone and brick*). To *alternate* is 'to do something by turns': *They alternated between urging us to go faster and telling us to slow down*. An *alternative* is 'another different thing that could act as a replacement': *an alternative venue*; *As an alternative to buying a new system, we could try to update the old one*.

In American English, however, *alternate* is widely used as an adjective in the sense of *alternative* (*an alternative venue*) and as a noun to mean 'a deputy or substitute'.

alternative or **alternate**? See **alternate** or **alternative**?

amend or **emend**? These two words are sometimes confused. To *amend* is a general word meaning to 'correct and improve': *She did her best to amend her behaviour*. It also has a specific meaning in relation to pieces of legislation, to 'alter or add to and improve' (*the Act of 1978 as amended in 1993*). *Emend* has a more limited use. It is used exclusively in relation to texts and means 'to remove errors or irregularities from' (*emended the text to bring it into line with modern spelling conventions*).

American Indian *American Indian* has been largely replaced by *Native American* as the preferred general name for a member of one of the indigenous peoples of, especially, North America. The terms *Indian* and *American Indian* are not considered intrinsically disrespectful, however, and are still quite frequently used by Native Americans themselves. See also **Native American**.

amiable or **amicable**? *Amiable*, meaning 'friendly and pleasant', is used mainly to describe people and their manner: *He seems a very amiable sort of fellow*. *Amicable*, meaning 'characterized by friendliness', refers chiefly to relationships and dealings between people: *reached an amicable settlement; Their relationship became more amicable once they had agreed the terms of the divorce*.

amicable or **amiable**? See **amiable** or **amicable**?

amoral or **immoral**? An *immoral* person is one who breaks accepted standards of right and wrong. To be *amoral* means that one rejects the whole concept of morality or does not know or cannot know right from wrong. Babies, animals, and robots could be said to be *amoral*.

an or **a**? See **a** or **an**?

ante- or **anti-**? These two prefixes are sometimes confused. *Ante-* means 'before' or 'in front of': *antechamber* ('a room leading into another room'); *antediluvian* ('before Noah's flood'; 'ridiculously outdated'); *antenatal* ('before birth'). The much commoner prefix *anti-* means 'in the opposite direction' or 'against' and can be, and is, attached to any number of words: *anticlockwise*; *antidepressant*; *anti-fox-hunting*. *Anti* (but not *ante*) can be used informally as a preposition (*I'm anti the whole idea*) or an adjective (*She's less anti now than when we first talked about the plan with her*).

anti- or **ante-**? See **ante-** or **anti-**?

antisocial, **asocial**, **non-social**, **unsociable** or **unsocial**? There are slight distinctions in meaning between these five related words that need to be observed. *Antisocial* means 'harmful to society': *antisocial behaviour*; *It's terribly antisocial to dump rubbish on the side of the road*. *Asocial* is a rarer word and implies total rejection, in this case of society or social contact – a recluse might be described as *asocial*. *Non-social* is used mainly as a technical term 'not socially oriented' – the life of many animal species could be described as *non-social*. To be *unsociable* usually means 'to be unfriendly and dislike company': *Our new neighbours are totally unsociable and have never even invited us in for a cup of tea*. In British English, *unsocial* is mainly found in the phrase *to work unsocial hours* meaning 'to work at times when most other people are at home'.

any *Any*, as a pronoun, may be used with a verb in either the singular or the plural: *I need some glue – is there any left?*; *We sold most of them, and any that were unsold we gave away to friends*. There is sometimes a subtle distinction in the choice of a singular or plural verb. *Is any of these seats free?* would mean, specifically, 'any one', whereas *Are any of these seats free?* could mean 'are some of them free?'

appraise or **apprise**? These two words are sometimes confused. To *appraise* is a fairly formal word meaning 'to assess' something or 'estimate its value': *appraise the damage caused by the fire*. To *apprise* is a very formal word meaning 'to inform' and is followed by the preposition *of*: *She had already apprised us of her intentions*.

apprise or **appraise**? See **appraise** or **apprise**?

apt, **liable**, and **likely** *Apt to*, *liable to*, and *likely to* are similar in meaning and use and need to be handled with care. *He is apt to exaggerate* means 'he often exaggerates (as we know from our experience of him)'; *he is likely to exaggerate* means 'he can be expected to exaggerate (in this instance)'. *He is liable to exaggerate* can mean either. When referring to a specific time in the future always use *likely*: *It is likely to rain tomorrow*. But *it is apt/liable/ likely to rain in November* means in all three forms 'November is often a rainy month'. See also **likely**.

Arab, **Arabian**, or **Arabic**? *Arab* is the correct adjective to use in political contexts: *Arab nations*; *an Arab leader*. The adjective *Arabian* is mainly used to designate things geographically as belonging to Arabia (the Arabian peninsula; lying between the Red Sea and the Persian Gulf): *in the Arabian desert*. *Arabic* refers principally to the language of the Arab peoples: *to learn Arabic*; *Arabic grammar*; *Arabic poetry*. The numbers in general world-wide use are *Arabic numerals*.

Arabian See **Arab**, **Arabian**, or **Arabic**?

Arabic See **Arab**, **Arabian**, or **Arabic?**

aren't *Aren't I?* is the standard less formal alternative for *am I not?*: *Aren't I clever to have thought of that?*; *I am on the list, aren't I?* It is incorrect to use *aren't* with *I* except in questions.

around, round, or **about**? *Round* is in standard use in British English as a preposition (*came round the corner*) or an adverb (*show someone round*), where American English would more commonly have *around*. It is not incorrect in British English either to use *around* in such phrases. Americans also tend to say *around* where most British users would say *about* (*Don't mess around/ about with my things; It must have taken around/about five hours*). Again, however, the use of *around* is quite common in British English and perfectly acceptable.

arrogate or **abrogate**? See **abrogate** or **arrogate**?

asocial See **antisocial**, **asocial**, **non-social**, **unsociable**, or **unsocial**?

assume or **presume**? *Assume* and *presume* are almost interchangeable in the meaning 'suppose'. *Presume* is rather more formal and tends to suggest that a supposition is made on the basis of a deduction or a reasonable likelihood, and has a slightly unfavourable tinge, possibly picked up from its other meaning ('to take liberties'): *Dr Livingstone, I presume?* (who else could it be?); *From what you said yesterday, I presumed that you'd already made up your mind. Assume* is, however, definitely the word to choose if something is being put forward as a basis for argument: *In drawing up your pension forecast, I assumed that interest rates would remain at about 5 per cent.*

assurance or **insurance**? British English uses the term *assurance* to refer to a form of insurance in which money is bound to be paid out at the end of a fixed period of time or on the death of the insured person: *life assurance. Insurance* is the general term covering all instances where money will only be paid in particular circumstances: *house contents insurance; travel insurance.*

assure, **ensure**, or **insure**? These three words are sometimes confused. The commonest meaning of the verb to *assure* is 'to inform (someone) positively': *I assured her that she had nothing to worry about*. *Assure* can also mean 'to make certain or safe' – but in this sense it is mainly found in the passive or adjectival form: *Their success is assured*; *Rest assured that we will do all we can to help you*. The verb generally used in the active form to mean 'make (something) certain' is *ensure* (often spelt *insure* in American English): *Our first duty is to ensure the safety of the passengers*. *Insure* refers simply to making arrangements to obtain financial compensation in the event of accident or loss: *The painting should be insured for at least a million pounds*.

aural or **oral**? These two words are pronounced the same and are easy to confuse. *Aural* relates to the ears and hearing and is connected with words such as *audible* and *audition*. An *aural* comprehension is one that tests a person's understanding of spoken language. *Oral* relates to the mouth and speaking. Students of foreign languages often have to take an *oral* examination, one that tests their ability to speak the language.

averse or **adverse**? See **adverse** or **averse**?

bacteria *Bacteria* is a plural noun and takes a plural verb. One single microorganism is a *bacterium*.

BC and **AD** See **AD** and **BC**.

beg the question Strictly speaking, a statement that *begs the question* is one that is logically flawed because it is based on an unproven assumption, often taking for granted the very thing that it itself is seeking to establish. If someone argues: *The Loch Ness monster must exist because there have been so many sightings* *of it*, that statement *begs the question* because it assumes that the sightings were of the monster and not something else – which is the whole point at issue. This is the original meaning of the phrase and the only one allowed by traditionalists. It is, however, probably more frequently used nowadays to mean that a statement raises obvious questions which need to be answered: *Their claim that the scheme will benefit millions begs the question of precisely what benefit those millions will receive*. While this use can reasonably be argued to have a link with the original meaning in that unwarranted assumptions are usually involved, the use of *begging the question* to mean simply that someone is 'avoiding the issue' or 'not giving a straight answer' is not recommended. There could be confusion with the strict sense and there are plenty of other phrases that unambiguously suggest that somebody is being evasive.

between you and me Prepositions are followed by the object form of the personal pronoun, not the subject form: *from me to him*; *for us and against them*. *Between* is no exception: *We divided it between us* (not *between we*). Having been told repeatedly that it is incorrect to say, for example, *You and me are two of a kind*, people sometimes overcorrect themselves and say *between you and I* when the grammatically correct form is *between you and me*.

billion A *billion* is nowadays generally understood to be 'one thousand million'. Formerly, this was the American understanding of the term. In British English a *billion* was formerly 'one million million'. Modern dictionaries now mark that sense of the term as dated or obsolete.

black, **Negro**, and **coloured** The word *black* (without a capital letter) is currently the most widely accepted non-offensive word for people of African or African-American origin. The terms *Negro* and *coloured*, which both formerly had this function, are no longer felt to be acceptable by black people themselves, although *Coloured* has a specific use in South Africa where it refers to members of a population group of mixed-race origin. Dark-skinned people of Asian origin should not be referred to as *black*, in the context of British society, but as *Asian*.

blatant or **flagrant**? These two words are close together in meaning, both indicating that something is openly outrageous. There is a difference of emphasis, however. *Blatant* emphasizes the obviousness of an offence: *It was such a blatant attempt at emotional blackmail that not even his doting mother could fail to see it.* *Flagrant*, on the other hand, emphasizes the offence's brazenly shocking or outrageous nature: *If they fail to condemn such a flagrant breach of the regulations, will they ever condemn anything at all?* Both words are spelt with two *a*'s.

blond or **blonde**? The two spellings, which are both correct, derive from the masculine (*blond*) and feminine (*blonde*) forms of the word in French. English tends to retain the distinction, at least to the extent of preferring the form *blonde* for women, about whom the word is most often used: *She's gone blonde; Gentlemen Prefer Blondes* (novel by Anita Loos). On this basis, it would be logical to write *He is blond* and *She has blonde hair* and to use *blond* in neutral contexts such as *blond-coloured wood*.

blonde or **blond**? See **blond** or **blonde**?

borrow See **lend**, **loan**, and **borrow**.

can or **may**? *Can* is nowadays used far more frequently than *may* when asking permission to do something (*Can I go now, please? Can we come too?*), and the battle by traditionalists to preserve a clear distinction between *can* 'be able to' and *may* 'be allowed to' has been effectively lost. *May* is however used in polite requests in formal contexts (*Professor Duckworth, may I present Dr Lowther?*), when the distinction between 'being able' and 'being allowed' is all-important (*It's not a question of whether he can do it, but whether he may*), and when *may* is needed to avoid ambiguity (*She knows perfectly well what she may and may not do*).

It should also be noted that *may* itself can be ambiguous. In a sentence such as *If the minister is satisfied that it is reasonable to do so, he may award a higher pension* it is unclear whether the minister will make the award because the regulations allow him to, or whether it is simply possible that he might make one.

cannon or **canon**? These two words are easily confused. The noun *cannon* means 'a large gun' or 'a shot in billiards or snooker'. *Cannon* is also a verb: *The shot cannoned off the far post. Canon* is only used as a noun and means 'a senior member of the clergy', 'a piece of music', 'a body of principles or rules', 'an authoritative list of books or authors' works'. The verb *canonize* is derived from it.

canon or **cannon**? See **cannon** or **canon**?

canvas or **canvass**? The material that tents are traditionally made of is *canvas*. Before an election, political parties *canvass* the voters to try to obtain their support.

canvass or **canvas**? See **canvas** or **canvass**?

Celsius or **centigrade**? *Celsius* has been internationally adopted as the name of the temperature scale and is always used, for example, in giving weather forecasts. *Centigrade* is no longer in technical use.

centigrade or **Celsius**? See **Celsius** or **centigrade**?

centre *Centre* is the correct British English spelling for both the noun and the verb; *center* is the equivalent spelling in American English. As a verb, *centre* ought logically to be followed by the prepositions *at*, *in*, *on*, or *upon*: *The debate centres on the issue of funding*. Despite its illogicality with respect to physical midpoints that cannot go around anything, the phrase *centre around* or *round* is well established and has been used by many respected writers such as Conrad and Kipling. Some traditionalists may prefer, however, to use another verb such as *revolve* in its place: *The whole debate revolves around the issue of funding*.

cereal or **serial**? These two words, which are pronounced the same, are sometimes confused. *Cereal* refers to grain and food (*breakfast cereal*; *cereal crops*). The word derives from the name of the Roman goddess of corn and agriculture *Ceres*, which is why it is spelt with two *e*'s. *Serial* derives from the word *series* and refers to things that happen in a series: *a serial killer*; *a TV serial*.

ceremonial or **ceremonious**? These two adjectives, both derived from *ceremony*, are sometimes confused. *Ceremonial* describes the nature of an occasion or thing, the fact that it is a ceremony or is used in ceremonies: *a ceremonial wreath-laying*; *ceremonial robes*. *Ceremonious* describes the elaborate and formal manner in which something is done: *a ceremonious bow*. People may be described as *ceremonious*, but not usually as *ceremonial*. *Ceremonial* is also used as a noun, meaning the elaborate and formal activity that usually accompanies a ceremony.

ceremonious or **ceremonial**? See **ceremonial** or **ceremonious**?

challenged The word *challenged* was put forward in the 1980s as a solution to the problem of how to describe, sensitively and positively, the various disabilities from which some people suffer – thus, *physically challenged* (disabled) and *visually challenged* (blind or with deficient eyesight). The word quickly came to be seen as a clear example of euphemism and political correctness and to be ridiculed in such combinations as *cerebrally challenged* (stupid) and *vertically challenged* (short). The question of how physical disabilities can be referred to in a way that is not demeaning to the sufferer is an ongoing one, but *challenged* is no longer recommended for serious use.

classic or **classical**? These two adjectives are not usually interchangeable in modern English. If something is described as *classic* it usually either sets a standard of excellence (*a classic recording*) or perfectly illustrates a particular phenomenon (*a classic case of mistaken identity*). *Classical* generally refers to the world of ancient Greece and Rome (*classical antiquity*), to serious music (*classical composers such as Beethoven and Mozart*), and to long-standing or formerly authoritative forms when contrasted with modern ones (*classical mechanics as opposed to quantum mechanics*). The distinction was considerably less clear-cut, however, in former times.

classical or **classic**? See **classic** or **classical**?

climactic or **climatic**? These two words are easily confused, but can be just as easily distinguished if the nouns they come from are borne in mind. *Climactic* comes from *climax*: *the climactic* *moment of the play. Climatic* comes from *climate*: *the climatic conditions in northern Borneo.*

climatic or **climactic**? See **climactic** or **climatic**?

coloured See **black**, **Negro**, and **coloured**.

common, **mutual**, or **reciprocal**? See **mutual**, **reciprocal**, or **common**?

compare to and **compare with** Both prepositions, *to* and *with*, can be used following *compare*. Neither is more correct than the other, but a slight distinction can be made in meaning. *To* has traditionally been preferred when the similarity between two things is the point of the comparison and *compare* means 'liken': *I hesitate to compare my own works to those of someone like Dickens.* *With*, on the other hand, suggests that the differences between two things are as important as, if not more important than, the similarities: *We compared the facilities available to most city-dwellers with those available to people living in the country; to compare like with like.* When *compare* is used intransitively, it should be followed by *with*: *Our output simply cannot compare with theirs.*

complement or **compliment**? See **compliment** or **complement**?

complement or **supplement**? Both these words convey the idea of adding something. If one thing *complements* another, however, it goes well with it and enhances it when they are put together: *A hat should complement the rest of one's outfit, not draw attention to itself.* If one thing *supplements* another, it adds to it and reinforces it: *She supplements her income by giving private music lessons.* A good wine may be a *complement* to a meal, but a person might need a dietary *supplement* if some essential element is lacking from the food they normally eat. Note that neither of these words is spelt with an *i*. See also **compliment** or **complement**?

complementary or **complimentary**? See **complimentary** or **complementary**?

compliment or **complement**? These two words are easily confused. An expression of admiration is a *compliment*: *My compliments to the chef; The remark was intended as a compliment*. A *complement* is an accompaniment to something that sets off its good qualities (*Wine is the perfect complement to a good meal*), or the full number of something (*the ship's complement* (the entire crew, officers and ordinary sailors); *had the usual complement of arms and legs*). The verbs *compliment* and *complement* work in the same way: *May I compliment you on your cooking?; Their characters may be different, but they complement each other well*. See also **complement** or **supplement**?

complimentary or **complementary**? There is the same difference in meaning between *complimentary* and *complementary* as between their respective nouns. A *complimentary* remark is flattering and expresses admiration. A *complimentary* ticket or *complimentary* copy of a book is given free as a mark of respect. *Complementary*, on the other hand, refers to the relationship between things or people that go well together: *complementary colours*.

comprise *Comprise* is a difficult word to use, because it is close in meaning to, but should be treated differently from, such verbs as *consist (of)*, *compose*, and *make up*. There are two rules to remember. First, a whole *comprises* (consists of or is composed of) its parts; the parts *make up* or *constitute* the whole, but do not *comprise* it: *The collection comprises over 500 items; The meal comprised no fewer than fifteen courses.* Secondly, *comprise* should not be followed by *of*, even when it is used in the passive.

confidante(e) or **confident**? A *confidant* is a person to whom one entrusts one's secrets. It is spelt *confidante* when the person in question is a woman or girl. *Confident* is the adjective meaning 'assured, certain': *We know we're facing tough opposition, but we're confident we can win.*

confident or **confidant(e)**? See **confidant(e)** or **confident**?

consensus The only *c* in *consensus* is at the beginning of the word – it is spelt with three *s*'s.

contagious or **infectious**? A *contagious* disease is spread by direct physical contact with an affected person or by touching something previously touched by an affected person: athlete's foot is a contagious disease. An *infectious* disease is transmitted by airborne microorganisms: chickenpox and influenza are highly *infectious* diseases.

continual or **continuous**? The classic illustration of the difference between these two closely related adjectives compares a dripping tap (*continual* – occurring constantly, again and again and again with breaks in between) with a flowing tap (*continuous* – continuing in an unbroken stream). It follows from this that *continual* is generally the word to use with a plural noun: (*continual interruptions; continual requests for this record*), whereas either word may accompany a singular noun: *a continual* (constantly renewed) or *continuous* (unceasing) *bombardment by the enemy.*

continuous or **continual**? See **continual** or **continuous**?

council or **counsel**? These two words, which are pronounced the same, are sometimes confused. A *council* is an administrative, advisory, or executive body of people: *stand for election to the local council; council workers*. A member of a *council* is a *councillor*. *Counsel* is a formal word for advice (*gave wise counsel*), and also means a lawyer or group of lawyers (*the counsel for the prosecution*). *Counsel* is also used as a verb meaning to 'advise', and a person who gives advice is a *counsellor*. Nowadays *counsel*, *counsellor*, and *counselling* are perhaps most frequently used in the context of professional help offered to people who have psychological, social, or personal problems or have had a traumatic experience: *Friends of the murdered teenager are being offered counselling*.

counsel or **council**? See **council** or **counsel**?

credible or **credulous**? These two words are sometimes confused. Something that is *credible* is believable: *His story seemed perfectly credible, if somewhat bizarre*. Someone who is *credulous*, on the other hand, is too ready to accept anything they are told as true: *Credulous punters were dazzled by promises of a 50 per cent return on their investments*.

credulous or **credible**? See **credible** or **credulous**?

crevasse or **crevice**? A *crevasse* is a large crack, for example in a mountain, glacier, or ice field. An unlucky mountaineer might fall down a *crevasse*. A *crevice* is a small or tiny crack, where dirt lodges or where one might lose a small coin.

crevice or **crevasse**? See **crevasse** or **crevice**?

criterion and **criteria** *Criteria* is the plural form of *criterion*. A phrase such as *this criteria* is incorrect. If a thing is judged by such and such *criteria*, then more than one standard of judgment is being applied to it: *Value for money is surely not the only relevant criterion in this case; The criteria by which schools will be judged to have succeeded or failed are set out in the report.*

currant or **current**? See **current** or **currant**?

current or **currant**? *Current* with an *e* has a wide range of meanings: *electric current; strong currents make swimming dangerous; current affairs; the current month. Currant* with an *a* is a fresh or dried berry: *redcurrants; currants and raisins.*

data *Data* is, strictly speaking, a plural noun with a comparatively rare singular form *datum*. With the advent of computers and data processing, *data* has come increasingly to be seen and used as a singular mass noun like *information* or *news*: *The data is currently being processed.* Traditionalists insist, however, that this should be: *The data are currently being processed.*

deceitful or **deceptive**? *Deceitful* implies an intention to deceive. Generally speaking, only people and their words and actions can be described as *deceitful. Deceptive* is applied to things that are able to mislead the unwary: *Appearances can be deceptive.*

deceptive or **deceitful**? See **deceitful** or **deceptive**?

decimate Historically, the word *decimate* refers to the practice in the Roman army of killing every tenth man in a mutinous unit in order to ensure loyalty of the surviving 90 per cent. Although the Latin word for 'tenth' is embedded in *decimate* (compare *decimal, decimetre*, etc.), the word is now accepted by all but the most historically minded as meaning 'kill or destroy a large number or part of something': *The famine decimated the population; The industry has been decimated.* It goes against the grain of the word, however, to link it with a specific quantity (*decimate by 50 per cent*), to apply it to an individual or indivisible thing, or to use it as a substitute for *annihilate* or *exterminate*.

defective or **deficient**? These two words are close together in meaning and can sometimes be used to describe the same thing, but there is a significant difference between them. *Defective* is applied to functioning things that fail to function properly: a *defective* component is faulty and does not work: *defective brakes*. *Deficient* primarily means 'lacking' or 'inadequate': *a diet deficient in the vitamins necessary for healthy growth*.

deficient or **defective**? See **defective** or **deficient**?

definite or **definitive**? These two words are sometimes confused. Both *definite* and *definitive* suggest that something is unlikely to be changed: a *definite* answer is clear, firm, and unambiguous; a *definite* date is one that has been decided on and fixed by the people involved. *Definitive* has connotations of being authoritative and conclusive: the *definitive* answer to a problem is one that solves it once and for all. If someone writes a *definitive* biography or gives us the *definitive* Hamlet, that person's book or performance becomes the standard by which all later ones are judged.

definitive or **definite**? See **definite** or **definitive**?

dependant or **dependent**? In British English *dependent* is an adjective (*dependent on her mother for support; too dependent on overseas imports*) and *dependant* is a noun meaning 'a dependent person' (*not earning enough to be able to provide adequately for her dependants*). In American English the form *dependent* is generally used both as an adjective and as a noun.

dependent or **dependant**? See **dependant** or **dependent**?

deprecate or **depreciate**? The difference in meaning of these two words is being eroded. To *deprecate* is a rather formal verb meaning to 'feel or express moral disapproval of (something)': *She deprecated their lack of courtesy towards the old lady*. To *depreciate* means both to 'fall in value' or 'lower the value of' (*The currency is depreciating*) and, more formally, to 'belittle (somebody or something)': *My efforts were depreciated and I was made to feel useless*. The distinction between expressing disapproval and belittling or disparaging is sometimes so fine that the words *deprecate* and *depreciate* are increasingly being used interchangeably.

depreciate or **deprecate**? See **deprecate** or **depreciate**?

derisive or **derisory**? See **derisory** or **derisive**?

derisory or **derisive**? These two words are sometimes confused. Both derive from the word *derision*. The main meaning of *derisory* in modern English is 'ridiculously small or inadequate' (and therefore deserving derision): *a derisory pay offer*. The only meaning of *derisive* is 'mocking' (expressing derision): *derisive jeers*.

desert or **dessert**? *Dessert* is a noun meaning 'the sweet course in a meal'. The stress in *dessert* is on the second syllable. A barren wilderness is a *desert* (a noun, with stress on the first syllable). The verb to *desert* (stress on the second syllable) means to 'abandon (somebody or something)' or to 'absent oneself from military duty without leave'. To *get one's just deserts* (plural noun, with stress on the second syllable) is to 'be treated as one deserves'.

despatch or **dispatch**? See **dispatch** or **despatch**?

dessert or **desert**? See **desert** or **dessert**?

dice and **die** Strictly and historically speaking, *dice* is the plural of *die*. The use of *dice* to mean a single small cube is, however, long established and perfectly acceptable. *Dice* therefore is both the singular and plural form: *to throw the dice* could refer to one or more cubes.

die and **dice** See **dice** and **die**.

different from/to/than The combination preferred by traditionalists is *different from*, which keeps *different* in line with to *differ* (*How does this version differ* (or *How is this version different*) *from the previous one?*). *Different to* has, however, been used for a very long time in British English, and most modern authorities on British English accept it as an alternative, at least in anything but very formal writing. *Different than* is in widespread use in American English and is cautiously accepted in British English when followed by a clause: *It's altogether different than I expected* (strictly: *different from what I expected*). *Different than* is not usually acceptable in either British or American English when followed by a noun.

dilemma Strictly, a *dilemma* refers to a situation in which one is faced by two, and only two, equally unpleasant alternatives – as in the slightly old-fashioned phrase *to be on the horns of a dilemma* or in the sentence *We are in a dilemma and can't decide whether to lower prices or risk losing sales*. A situation where there are more than two unpleasant alternatives is, strictly speaking, a *quandary*, though many dictionaries define a *dilemma* as involving 'two or more' unpleasant alternatives. *Dilemma* ought not to be used in careful writing if there is an open choice as to how to deal with a problem or if the alternatives faced are not unpleasant.

disc or **disk**? *Disc* is the correct spelling of the word in British English, except in the context of computers where the usual American English spelling *disk* is generally preferred: *a slipped disc* but *a disk drive*.

discomfit or **discomfort**? *Discomfit* originally meant to 'defeat' and from that came to mean to 'thwart': *His attempts at persuasion were of no avail and he retired discomfited*. Because it is usually pronounced the same, or virtually the same way as the commoner and weaker verb *discomfort*, it is now often treated as having the same meaning to 'make (someone) feel uneasy'. Careful users might feel that *discomfort* expresses this idea perfectly adequately and that it is worth keeping the older meaning of *discomfit* alive.

discomfort or **discomfit**? See **discomfit** or **discomfort**?

discreet or **discrete**? Though they are pronounced the same and look very similar, these two words have distinct and different meanings. When used of people, *discreet* means 'careful, reliable, and not likely to gossip' (*Can we rely on her to be discreet?*); when used about actions, it means 'unlikely to attract attention' (*We have made a few discreet enquiries*). *Discrete* is a more technical word meaning 'separate' or 'individually distinct': *The process can be broken down into a number of discrete stages*.

discrete or **discreet**? See **discreet** or **discrete**?

disinterested or **uninterested**? *Disinterested* is now so often used to mean 'unconcerned' or 'bored' (in other words *uninterested*), that it can easily be misinterpreted when used in its primary meaning in modern English of 'impartial' or 'not motivated by selfishness'. A *disinterested* observer is somebody who is not on anybody's side; an *uninterested* observer simply does not care about what is going on. Careful users of English should try to preserve this distinction.

disk or **disc**? See **disc** or **disk**?

disorient or **disorientate**? Both forms of the word are correct. *Disorient* is more often used in American English, *disorientate* in British English.

disorientate or **disorient**? See **disorient** or **disorientate**?

dispatch or **despatch**? Both spellings are equally acceptable; *dispatch* is the commoner of the two.

distinct or **distinctive**? These two words are sometimes confused. *Distinct* means 'clear', 'clearly noticeable' or 'separate and different': *a distinct air of unease*; *The word has two distinct meanings*. Something that is *distinctive* has its own special and unmistakable character: *a distinctive flavour*.

distinctive or **distinct**? See **distinct** or **distinctive**?

dived and **dove** *Dove* is an alternative past tense form of to *dive* in American English. It is not used in British English.

double negative The use of *not* together with another negative word as in *I don't know nothing* is not standard English. A less glaring error, but still an error, is the use of the second *not* in *It wouldn't surprise me if it didn't rain*. There the second *not* is simply superfluous: *It wouldn't surprise me if it rained* or, with a different emphasis, *It would surprise me if it didn't rain*.

Double negative forms may be used when the intention is to express a positive idea: *a not unusual* (quite common) *request*; *not unrelated* (there may be a link); *not infrequently* (quite often);

One simply cannot not be impressed (one cannot fail to be). The *not un-* construction is often used to express a slight reservation in the speaker's mind (*Let's say that it was not unimpressive*) and is useful for that purpose. The *cannot not* construction is usually best replaced by something less ungainly: *cannot but be impressed*; *cannot fail to be impressed*. Occasionally more than two negatives in a sequence are encountered: '*This does not imply that sexual relations that don't risk conception are unrelated to personal responsibility and morality*' (Margaret Drabble).

dove and **dived** See **dived** and **dove**.

due to or **owing to**? The traditional rule of thumb regarding the use of these two phrases is that *owing to* means and can be replaced in a sentence by 'because of', while *due to* means and is replaceable by 'caused by': *Owing to circumstances beyond our control, the departure of the train has had to be delayed*; *The delay is due to circumstances beyond our control*. The basis for this rule is said to be that *due* is an adjective and ought either to be attached to a noun (*a mistake due to ignorance*) or to follow a verb such as *to be* or *to seem*: *Her mistakes were mainly due to inexperience*. *Owing to*, on the other hand, is said to be a compound preposition that can introduce an adverbial phrase: *cancelled owing to rain*; *Owing to an earlier engagement, I reluctantly had to turn down the invitation*. Most modern authorities recommend that the rule should be remembered, while acknowledging that its grammatical basis is shaky (there is no reason why *due to* should not be seen as a compound preposition if *owing to* is one) and that *due to* is so frequently used in the sense of *because of* that many modern dictionaries show it with that sense.

dumb The use of *dumb* in the originally American and informal sense of 'stupid' has become so widespread that great care should be taken with the use of the word in its basic sense 'unable to speak'. If there is any risk of misunderstanding or offence, a word such as *mute* or *speech-impaired* should be used instead.

each other or **one another**? The traditional rule states that *each other* refers to a relationship between only two people or things (*We love each other and want to get married*), whereas *one another* refers to a relationship between more than two people (*Christ commanded his disciples to love one another*). Modern authorities point out, however, that there is no basis for this rule except tradition and there can be no objection in principle to sentences such as *Harris and Jones mistrusted their boss even more than they mistrusted one another* or *All members of this organization are expected to help each other.*

eatable or **edible**? Both *eatable* and *edible* mean 'reasonably pleasant to eat': *If you put plenty of sauce on it, it's just about eatable* or *edible*. The primary meaning of *edible*, however, is 'possible to eat', 'non-poisonous': *Are these berries edible?*

economic or **economical**? *Economic* means first 'relating to economics or an economy' (*an economic crisis; economic indicators*), secondly 'reasonably profitable' (*If the price of tin were to rise, it might become economic to reopen the mine*), and thirdly 'not wasteful'. This third meaning overlaps with that of *economical* (*an economical* or *economic use of resources*). *Economical* is, however, far more widely and commonly used in this sense. A person who is thrifty or a machine that uses resources frugally should be described by preference as *economical*: *a very economical little car.*

economical or **economic**? See **economic** or **economical**?

edible or **eatable**? See **eatable** or **edible**?

effect or **affect**? See **affect** or **effect**?

e.g. or **i.e.**? The abbreviation *e.g.* means 'for example' (Latin *e*xempli *g*ratia) and usually introduces a brief list of things or people to illustrate a concept: *a computer peripheral, e.g. a printer or a scanner*. The abbreviation *i.e.* means 'that is' (Latin *id* *e*st). It usually introduces a brief amplification or explanation of a concept: *a computer peripheral, i.e. a device such as a printer or scanner that is connected up to a computer*.

egoism or **egotism**? The difference between these two words in ordinary use is slight, both being used as equivalents to self-centredness. The more technical uses of the two words give a clue to where the distinction should lie. *Egoism* is also a philo-sophical belief in selfishness as the only real (and only proper) motive for action: *egotism* is self-obsession, for example the excessive use of *I*, *me*, and *myself* when speaking. *Egoism* is, therefore, best used for *self-seeking* and *egotism* for *self-importance*.

egotism or **egoism**? See **egoism** or **egotism**?

either *Either*, when it is the subject of a sentence, should be fol-lowed by a verb in the singular: *Either of the plans is acceptable*. If both subjects are singular, a singular verb should be used (*Either Peter or Andrew is intending to come*) and if both subjects are plural, a plural verb should be used (*Either relatives or friends are welcome*). Where there is a combination of singular and plural subjects, it is best to let the form of the second one determine the form of the verb: *Either he or you have to go*. See also pp. 10–13.

elder or **older**? *Elder* is used only in comparing the ages of people, usually within a family group (*my elder brother/sister*), and cannot be followed by *than* (*My brother is two years older* – not *elder – than I am*). *Older* can be used in place of *elder* and is always used when describing things.

electric or **electrical**? *Electric* is the adjective generally used to describe specific things that carry or are powered by electricity: *an electric circuit; an electric motor; an electric toothbrush. Electrical* tends to be used with more general or abstract nouns: *an electrical appliance; electrical goods; electrical engineering.* There is, however, a good deal of overlap. *Electric* is the adjective usually used in figurative contexts: *The atmosphere was electric*.

electrical or **electric**? See **electric** or **electrical**?

elicit or **illicit**? These two words are sometimes confused. *Elicit* is a verb, usually followed by the preposition *from* meaning 'to call or draw forth (something)': *We managed to elicit from him how he obtained the information. Illicit* is an adjective meaning 'illegal' or 'not allowed': *an illicit love affair*.

embarrass *Embarrass* is spelt with two *r*'s and two *s*'s.

emend or **amend**? See **amend** or **emend**?

emotional or **emotive**? See **emotive** or **emotional**?

emotive or **emotional**? The main meaning of *emotive* is 'arousing strong feelings, appealing to the feelings (rather than reason)': an *emotive* issue is one which people get very worked up about, an *emotive* use of language chooses words specifically for their power to produce an *emotional* response. *Emotional* is the commoner word with a broader range of use; its core sense is 'feeling or expressing emotion'. An *emotional* person is one who is readily affected by and inclined to show emotion. *He made an emotional speech* would mean that the speaker showed in his speech how strongly he himself felt about something. *She made an emotive speech* would suggest that she was more interested in stirring up the crowd than expressing her own feeling.

enormity In modern English *enormity* means both 'huge size' (*the enormity of the task*) and 'outrageousness' or 'an outrageous crime' (*How could such an apparently innocuous person be guilty of these enormities?*). The second and third senses are the older-established ones (though probably less common now), and traditionalists think that the meaning 'huge size' should be rendered either by *enormousness* or another word such as *vastness* or *immensity*.

enquire or **inquire**? *Enquire* is the commoner British English spelling; *inquire* is generally used in American English. Some British users distinguish between *enquire* ('ask') and *inquire* (into) ('investigate'), but there are no strong grounds for making this distinction.

ensure, assure, or **insure**? See **assure, ensure,** or **insure**?

envelop or **envelope**? These two words are related and sometimes confused. *Envelop* (always pronounced with the stress on the second syllable *-vel-*) is a verb: *Fog envelops the city; enveloped in a huge black cloak. Envelope* (always pronounced with the stress on the first syllable *en-*) is the noun: *She opened the sealed envelope and drew out the winner's name.*

envelope or **envelop**? See **envelop** or **envelope**?

envisage or **envision**? These two words are similar in meaning, with the sense of to 'form a mental image of (something) in advance': *The group envisages a future in which all farming will be organic*. *Envisage* is more commonly used in British English; *envision* in American English. The meaning is quite close to that of *expect*, but the distinction should be preserved, and *expect* should be used in place of *envisage* in sentences such as *A further fall in interest rates is expected* – not *envisaged* – *next month*.

envision or **envisage**? See **envisage** or **envision**?

equable or **equitable**? These two words are sometimes confused. *Equable* means 'even-tempered' or 'free from extremes' and is frequently used to describe a person's character: *He has a very equable temperament*. *Equitable* means 'fair' or 'just': *an equitable system of taxation*.

equitable or **equable**? See **equable** or **equitable**?

erupt or **irrupt**? These two words are closely related and pronounced the same, but have distinct meanings. *Erupt* is much the commoner word and its basic meaning, taken from Latin, is 'break out' (volcanoes and skin rashes *erupt*), while the basic meaning of *irrupt* is 'break in': *He irrupted into the room demanding to know the whereabouts of his fiancée*. Generally speaking, *erupt* is the verb to use in figurative senses: *Violence erupted in the streets*; *When presented with the bill, she immediately erupted*.

Eskimo or **Inuit**? See **Inuit** or **Eskimo**?

especially or **specially**? There is some overlap in the meaning of these two words, but there are also areas in which their meanings should be distinguished. *Especially* means both 'very' (*an especially nice surprise*) and 'above all' (*I was impressed with all the performances, especially Nigel's*). *Specially* means 'in a special way' (*specially cooked using a totally new method*) and, more commonly, 'specifically, for a particular purpose' (*specially trained staff; I specially arranged it so that you would be in the same group as Jean*). In a sentence such as the following, however, either *especially* or *specially* could be used: *I made it especially* (or *specially*) *for you.*

-ess As part of the movement to eliminate sexism from language and from people's thinking, the use of the feminizing suffix *-ess* (and similar suffixes such as *-ette* and *-trix*) came, in the late twentieth century, to be seen as inappropriate and patronizing. The 'male' term is treated as a neutral term with no sexual reference. A woman author should therefore be referred to as an *author*, not an *authoress*, a woman editor as an *editor*, not an *editress* or *editrix*, etc. However, a few forms are retained. Female titles of nobility such as *countess* or *baroness* are still correct. *Manageress* is acceptable when referring to a woman who runs a shop, but not when referring to a woman company executive. A *priestess* is a woman priest of a pre-Christian religion, not an ordained Christian minister.

etc. The full form of *etc.* is traditionally written as two words *et cetera*, though the one-word variant is now equally acceptable. The first word or syllable of *et cetera* should be pronounced *et* (as in *pet*), not *ek*.

-ever, ever *Whoever, however, whatever*, etc. are written as one word when they mean 'any person who', 'in whichever way', or 'no matter what': *However you decide to do it, make sure you get it done quickly.* But when *ever* is used with a word like *who, how*, or *what* in the intensifying sense of 'on earth', the two words are written separately: *Who ever can it be?*; *What ever did he mean by that?*

exceptionable or **exceptional**? See **exceptional** or **exceptionable**?

exceptional or **exceptionable**? These two words are sometimes confused. *Exceptional* means 'outstanding' (*an exceptional student*) or 'extremely unusual' (*only under exceptional circumstances*). *Exceptionable* is a formal word meaning 'objectionable', 'offensive': *I was not the only one who found her remarks exceptionable*. See also **unexceptional** or **unexceptionable**?

expedient or **expeditious**? *Expedient* means 'useful or convenient in the circumstances (often disregarding moral considerations)': *It might be expedient to deny any knowledge of the plan*. It is also a noun meaning 'a useful or convenient action or plan': *a short-term expedient to get us out of difficulty*. It is sometimes confused with *expeditious*, which is a formal word meaning 'quick and efficient': *the most expeditious method of sending supplies*.

expeditious or **expedient**? See **expedient** or **expeditious**?

extant or **extinct**? Though rather similar in spelling, these two words have opposite meanings. *Extant* is a rather formal word meaning 'still in existence': *the only extant copy of the document*. Something that is *extinct* is no longer in existence: *The species is in danger of becoming extinct*.

extinct or **extant**? See **extant** or **extinct**?

factious or **fractious**? These two words are sometimes confused.

Factious means 'caused by or producing dissension within a larger body such as a political party; divisive': *factious infighting*. *Fractious* means 'unruly' or 'quarrelsome': *a fractious three-year-old*.

faint or **feint**? In the sense of paper with pale horizontal rulings, either spelling may be used, but *feint* is the preferred form: *A4 narrow feint margin paper*.

farther or **further**? These two spellings are sometimes confused. When referring to physical distance, *farther* and *further* are equally correct: *Penzance lies farther* (or *further*) *west than Truro*. In abstract and figurative senses, *further* is the preferred form: *of no further use; closed until further notice*. As a verb, only *further* is used: *to further God's purposes*.

fatal or **fateful**? These two words are sometimes confused. *Fatal* means 'causing or resulting in death': *a fatal accident* or 'causing ruin; ending in disaster': *a fatal mistake*. *Fateful* means 'momentously important': *their fateful meeting*. In the sense of 'having significant, often unpleasant consequences' either word may be used, although *fateful* is more usual: *that fateful day*. Care should be taken to avoid misinterpretation: a *fateful* experiment may change lives; a *fatal* experiment may lead to death.

fateful or **fatal**? See **fatal** or **fateful**?

feasible *Feasible* means 'able to be done or capable of being dealt with': *a feasible project*. Its use to mean 'likely' or 'probable' (*a feasible explanation of the events*) is best avoided.

feint or **faint**? See **faint** or **feint**?

female or **feminine**? *Female* is used to describe the sex that bears offspring or produces eggs, and plants or flowers that produce seeds: *a female deer is called a doe*. *Feminine* is used only of human beings, not plants or animals, and describes qualities and behaviour that are traditionally ascribed to women rather than men: *feminine charm*. *Feminine* is also used in some languages to describe nouns, adjectives, and pronouns in contrast to those that are masculine or neuter.

feminine or **female**? See **female** or **feminine**?

ferment or **foment**? Either of these two verbs may be used in the sense 'to rouse or incite a state of agitation': *to ferment/foment rebellion*. In their literal senses, the verbs differ: *foment* means 'to apply a hot moist substance to the body' and *ferment* 'to (cause to) undergo a chemical change with the release of bubbles of gas'.

fewer or **less**? The general rule is to use *fewer* with plural nouns (*fewer people, fewer books*) and *less* with singular nouns (*less time, less work, less sugar*). More precisely, *fewer* is used with people or things that can be counted (*fewer than 100 people came to the meeting*) and *less* is used with quantities and numbers that give a quantity or size: *less than two years ago*. The use of *less* with plural nouns should be avoided: *fewer opportunities*, not *less opportunities*. This incorrect usage is, however, frequently found in informal contexts.

fictional or **fictitious**? These two words are sometimes confused. *Fictional* means 'of fiction': *fictional heroes*; *fictitious* means 'not real or genuine; false': *He gave a fictitious name to the police*.

fictitious or **fictional**? See **fictional** or **fictitious**?

fish Traditionally, the plural form of *fish* is *fish*: *He caught several*

fish between 3lb and 7lb in weight; Two rounds of fish and chips.
The plural *fishes* is mainly used when describing different species
and in technical contexts: *marine fishes such as the mullet and sea
moth.*

flagrant or **blatant**? See **blatant** or **flagrant**?

flair or **flare**? These two words, which are pronounced the same,
are sometimes confused. A *flair* is a natural aptitude or talent,
especially one in which intuitive discernment is shown: *a flair
for speaking foreign languages.* A *flare* is a device that produces a
sudden blaze of light (*fired a flare so that the rescue party could
find them*) or a part that spreads outwards (*trousers with wide
flares*).

flammable or **inflammable**? Although *flammable* and *inflammable* may appear to be opposites, in fact they have the same
meaning. Since *inflammable* may seem to mean 'not flammable'
(from the prefix *in-* meaning 'not' + *flammable*) and because of
the risk of fire and danger to life, use of the word *flammable* is
increasingly preferred, especially in technical contexts: *highly
flammable solvents.* The preferred negative is *non-flammable*: *non-
flammable clothing.*

flare or **flair**? See **flair** or **flare**?

flaunt or **flout**? These two words are sometimes confused. To
flaunt means 'to display ostentatiously': *to flaunt one's superiority;
to flaunt one's wealth*; *flout* means 'to treat with contemptuous
disregard': *flout one's parents' wishes*; *The present laws are widely
flouted.* The verb *flaunt* is sometimes incorrectly used for *flout*:
to flaunt the rules and *to flaunt convention* are wrong.

flounder or **founder**? *Flounder* means to struggle to move (*floun-*

dering in the mud); founder when referring to a ship means 'to sink' and when referring to an animal means 'to go lame'. In their extended senses these two words are sometimes confused, but it is helpful to maintain the following distinctions: *founder* implies complete failure: *The plans foundered after attempts to raise money failed;* while someone who *flounders* is struggling awkwardly: *flounder through a speech.*

flout or **flaunt**? See **flaunt** or **flout**?

foment or **ferment**? See **ferment** or **foment**?

for- or **fore-**? These two prefixes are sometimes confused. The prefix *for-* denotes prohibition (*forbid*) or omission (*forsake*). The prefix *fore-* means 'before' (*foresee*). See also **forbear** or **forebear**?; **forego** or **forgo**?

forbear or **forebear**? The verb that means 'refrain from' is spelt *forbear*, with *bear* stressed (*forbore to reply to the accusation*); the noun that means 'ancestor' is spelt either *forebear* or *forbear*, with *for(e)* stressed.

fore- or **for-**? See **for-** or **fore**?

forebear or **forbear**? See **forbear** or **forebear**?

forego or **forgo**? The spelling *forego*, meaning 'to go before', is usually only found in the forms *foregoing* (*The foregoing remarks apply in all instances*) and *foregone* (*The victory was a foregone conclusion*). *Forgo*, more rarely spelt *forego*, is a different verb that means 'to refrain from': *The country decided to forgo its right to intervene.*

for ever or **forever**? When the meaning is 'for all future time' the spelling as two words is preferred: *I will love you for ever.*

When the meaning is 'constantly; with persistence' the spelling as one word is more common: *The children are forever asking me for money.*

forever or **for ever**? See **for ever** or **forever**?

forgo or **forego**? See **forego** or **forgo**?

former and **latter** The *former* refers back to the first of two previously mentioned things or people, the *latter* to the second. They are used to avoid tedious or awkward repetition: *Given the choice of being vilified by a newspaper or being ignored by it, I would instinctively opt for the former.* They should never be used when more than two things are listed. In that case use *first, first-named, second, last*, etc. They should also be avoided when it is not absolutely and immediately clear what they refer to.

fortuitous or **fortunate**? Primarily, and from its origins, *fortuitous* means 'occurring by chance': *I had no idea she was going to be there; our meeting was entirely fortuitous.* In modern writing and speech *fortuitous* has also come to refer to things that happen by good fortune, not simply by chance (*The event could not have happened at a more fortuitous time*), but this is a usage that traditionalists seek to avoid. *Fortunate*, by contrast, means 'lucky' or 'auspicious'.

fortunate or **fortuitous**? See **fortuitous** or **fortunate**?

founder or **flounder**? See **flounder** or **founder**?

fractious or **factious**? See **factious** or **fractious**?

-ful The standard modern way of forming the plural of nouns ending in *-ful* is simply to add *-s* to the end of the word: *handfuls*, *pocketfuls*, *cupfuls*, *spoonfuls*. It is generally preferable to the alternative way, where -*s* is added to the end of the first element (*handsful*, *pocketsful*), which may seem quaint or pedantic.

fulsome In its standard modern meaning, *fulsome* is a strongly uncomplimentary word. *Fulsome praise* is embarrassingly excessive or insincerely flattering. Though *fulsome* derives originally from a word meaning 'abundant', its use in a positive sense to mean 'copious', 'very full', or 'lavish' should be avoided for fear of misunderstanding.

further or **farther**? See **farther** or **further**?

gay The primary meaning of *gay* in contemporary English is 'homosexual'. As an adjective or a noun, it is the standard term used by homosexuals to describe themselves and as such has become part of the standard vocabulary of world English. This development has only occurred since the 1960s. Before then, in standard usage, *gay* was an adjective meaning 'cheerful' or 'bright'. These senses are still sometimes used, but care should be taken when using the word with these meanings to avoid misunderstanding.

gender and **sex** Efforts have been made in recent years to enforce a distinction between *gender* and *sex*, using *gender* to refer to femaleness or maleness in cultural, social, and linguistic contexts and *sex* in biological ones. This distinction is far from being universally applied or accepted, and it is still perfectly in order to speak of 'sex roles' or 'sexual stereotypes'. *Gender* should, however, be used where there is a risk of *sex* being misunderstood to mean 'sexual activity' rather than maleness or femaleness. *Gender* is the correct term to use in language contexts when classifying nouns as masculine, feminine, or neuter.

gibe, **gybe**, or **jibe**? *Gibe* means 'a taunting comment' or 'to jeer'. *Gybe* is a technical term in sailing meaning 'to change tack' or (of a sail) 'to swing sideways across the boat'. In British and American English *jibe* is an alternative spelling for *gibe*. In American English *jibe* is also an alternative spelling for *gybe*, besides having a separate meaning 'to accord with'.

gotten The form *gotten* as a past participle of *get* is not used in British English but is common in American English, although often considered to be non-standard. In American English *gotten* is generally used when the sense is 'obtained or acquired': *She's gotten herself a new apartment*, and the past participle *got* may be used when the sense is 'possessed', though Americans usually use *have*: *We already have one*; *We've already got one*.

    -*gotten* is standard in British English in *ill-gotten*: *ill-gotten gains*.

gourmand or **gourmet**? These two words are often confused. A *gourmand* is somebody who eats large or excessive amounts of food. It is not a complimentary word. A *gourmet*, on the other hand, is a complimentary word that refers to somebody with a refined taste in food, whose interest is in quality not quantity.

gourmet or **gourmand**? See **gourmand** or **gourmet**?

graceful or **gracious**? These two words are sometimes confused. Both derive from the noun *grace*, but pick up different senses of that word. *Graceful* usually refers to physical movement or shape (*a graceful dancer*; *the slim, graceful curves of the yacht*). When applied to moral actions (*a graceful apology*), it implies kindness or generosity as well as social deftness. *Gracious* is only used of people's characters or moral acts and usually implies that a person of superior standing is showing kindness, generosity, or mercy to someone of lower status (*by gracious permission of Her Royal Highness*).

gracious or **graceful**? See **graceful** or **gracious**?

graffiti *Graffiti* is a plural noun and should, theoretically, always be followed by a plural verb. It comes from Italian and has a regular Italian singular form, *graffito*. In English, however, the singular form is rare and its use is apt to seem pedantic. The form *graffiti* is therefore commonly used with a singular verb to refer to a single drawing (*a graffiti*) or to drawings collectively: *Graffiti is a good way of telling people your message.*

gray or **grey**? See **grey** or **gray**?

grey or **gray**? *Grey* is the correct spelling in British English; *gray* is the correct spelling for the same word in American English.

grill or **grille**? A set of metal bars on which food is cooked is a *grill*. A restaurant serving grilled food is a *grill*, and the upper heating element in a cooker is also a *grill*. Either spelling, however, can be used when the word means a mesh or grating, for example, on the front of a car (*a radiator grille* or, less commonly, *grill*).

grille or **grill**? See **grill** or **grille**?

gybe, **gibe**, or **jibe**? See **gibe**, **gybe**, or **jibe**?

hail or **hale**? These two words, which are pronounced the same, are sometimes confused. To *hail* someone or something is to call out to them or summon them (*hail a taxi*), or to acclaim them (*hailed as the new Fred Astaire; hail, Caesar!*). To *hail* from a place is to come or originate from it. Icy raindrops fall as *hail*, and someone can *hail* missiles or abuse down on someone else.

To *hale* is a rather literary or old-fashioned verb meaning to haul or to compel to come (*haled him before the magistrate*). As an adjective, *hale* means 'in good health' (*hale and hearty*).

hale or **hail**? See **hail** or **hale**?

hanged or **hung**? *Hung* is the correct form of the past tense and past participle of *to hang*, except in the sense 'to execute by hanging'. In this sense the form *hanged* (*was hanged at Tyburn*) is preferable, although *hung* is often found (*hung, drawn, and quartered*). *Hanged* is always used for a mild rather dated oath: (*I'll be*) *hanged if I know!*

hardly *Hardly* should not be used as the adverbial form of *hard*; *hard* itself performs this function (*hit someone hard*; *be hard pressed*). *Hardly* means the same as *barely* or *scarcely* and, like them, has an in-built negative effect, so that *I can hardly see* and *hardly anything* are correct, and *I can't hardly see* and *nothing hardly* are incorrect. When *hardly* begins a sentence, the usual order of auxiliary verb and subject is reversed: *Hardly had the meeting begun, when trouble erupted*. Note that the clause following this construction should begin with *when* or *before*, not *than*.

Hindi or **Hindu**? These two words are sometimes confused. *Hindi* is a language spoken in northern India and is one of India's two official languages. A *Hindu* is a follower of Hinduism, the main religion of India.

Hindu or **Hindi**? See **Hindi** or **Hindu**?

historic or **historical**? These two words are sometimes confused. A *historic* event is one that is very important or memorable and thought likely to be recorded as such in history. A *historical* event is any event that took place in the past.

historical or **historic**? See **historic** or **historical**?

hoard or **horde**? These two words are pronounced the same but have different meanings. A *hoard* is a store or collection, often of valuable things (*a pirate's hoard*). A *horde* is a large and sometimes unruly group of people (*resorts overrun by hordes of tourists*).

homely or **homy**? In British English, *homely* means 'reminiscent of home and the simple life' – familiar, unpretentious, or sympathetic and kind. In American English, however, its main meaning is 'not good-looking' (*She didn't look like a film star, in fact she was downright homely*). The word *homy* (usually *homey* in American English) means 'comfortable and relaxed, like a home' (*a homy atmosphere*).

homy or **homely**? See **homely** or **homy**?

hopefully Though the use of *hopefully* as a sentence adverb in the sense, 'it is to be hoped (that); let us hope' in sentences such as *Hopefully, they'll be home before it gets dark* is still decried by traditionalists in Britain and America, it has generally established itself as part of normal usage. It is interesting to note, however, that opposition to such words as *thankfully* and *regrettably* with a similar function has not been expressed. So while it may appear unnecessarily restrictive to reserve the use of the word to such constructions as *She eyed the plate of jam tarts hopefully* it is probably better to limit the sentence adverb use of *hopefully* to informal or spoken contexts.

Care should be taken over the position of *hopefully*. When *hopefully* is placed immediately in front of the verb, ambiguity may result: *They will hopefully wait for an answer* may mean either 'I hope they will wait for an answer' or 'they will wait for an answer with hope'. *Hopefully they will wait for an answer* and *They will wait for an answer hopefully* are less ambiguous.

horde or **hoard**? See **hoard** or **horde**?

human or **humane**? *Human* means 'belonging or relating to human beings as a race' (*human nature, human society*). *Humane* has a more limited use. It means 'showing compassion or kindness' (*humane treatment of animals*) or, more rarely, 'culturally broad and liberal' (*a humane education*).

humane or **human**? See **human** or **humane**?

hung or **hanged**? See **hanged** or **hung**?

hyper- or **hypo-**? These two prefixes are easily confused. *Hyper-* means 'excessively' or 'higher than normal': *hypercritical, hypersensitive, hyperinflation; hypertension* is abnormally high blood pressure. *Hypo-* means 'below' or 'less than normal': a *hypodermic* needle pierces beneath the skin; *hypotension* is abnormally low blood pressure. Note that someone who is exposed to extreme cold suffers from *hypothermia*. The word *hyperthermia* also exists, but refers to a condition in which the body temperature is abnormally high.

hypo- or **hyper-**? See **hyper-** or **hypo-**?

i.e. or **e.g.**? See **e.g.** or **i.e.**?

if and **whether** *If* and *whether* can often be used interchangeably: *He asked if* (or *whether*) *he could come too; I doubt whether* (or *if*) *we'll have time*. *Whether* should be preferred in more formal writing, however, and where there is a danger that using *if* could be ambiguous. *Let me know if he calls* could mean 'tell me that he's calling, when and if he calls' or 'tell me (afterwards) whether he called or not'.

illicit or **elicit**? See **elicit** or **illicit**?

immoral or **amoral**? See **amoral** or **immoral**?

immunity or **impunity**? *Immunity* and *impunity* have similar meanings and should not be confused. *Immunity* means a state of being protected against or exempt from something that could affect others: *immunity from a disease, immunity from prosecution. Impunity* has a more restricted use and is almost always found in the phrase *with impunity*, meaning 'without suffering punishment or bad consequences': *Are we going to let them break all the rules with impunity?*

impact Many traditionalists dislike the use of the verb *impact on* in figurative contexts – *Higher interest rates have impacted on consumer spending* – preferring the use of such verbs as *affect* or *influence* instead. *Impact* is pronounced differently depending on whether it is used as a noun or a verb. The stress in *impact* the noun (*braced themselves for the impact*) is on the first syllable *im-*. The stress in verbal use (*How will this impact on our plans for expansion?*) is on the second syllable.

imperial or **imperious**? *Imperial* means 'relating to an empire or emperor' (*an imperial edict; imperial robes*). *Imperious* refers to a person's character or behaviour and is usually uncomplimentary; it means 'haughty' or 'overbearing' (*demanding in an imperious tone to be served immediately*).

imperious or **imperial**? See **imperial** or **imperious**?

impinge or **infringe**? *Impinge* is a formal word meaning 'to affect' (often adversely) and is always followed by the preposition *on* or *upon*: *impinge upon someone's private life. Infringe* is often used in the same way and with the same meaning: *infringe on the rights of others. Infringe* is also and, according to some traditionalists, more properly used with a direct object meaning 'to violate': *to infringe the regulations/a patent/someone's rights.*

imply or **infer**? These two words are sometimes confused, though they in fact are opposite in meaning. To *imply* something is to suggest it by what you say without stating it explicitly: *She implied that I was untrustworthy.* To *infer* something is to deduce it from what someone says, even though they have not explicitly said as much: *I inferred from her remark that she thought me untrustworthy.* That said, the use of *infer* to mean the same as *imply* has become increasingly common.

impracticable or **impractical**? See **impractical** or **impracticable**?

impractical or **impracticable**? These two words are very close in meaning, but it is useful to distinguish between them. A plan that is *impractical* may be fine in theory but is difficult to carry out or of little use in practice. An *impracticable* plan is, quite simply, impossible to carry out. A person can be described as *impractical* ('not good at ordinary tasks' or 'not down-to-earth'), but not as *impracticable*.

impunity or **immunity**? See **immunity** or **impunity**?

inapt or **inept**? These two words are close together in meaning and sometimes confused. *Inapt* means 'inappropriate' (*an inapt quotation*); *inept* means 'clumsy' or 'incompetent'. A person can be described as *inept* but not, usually, as *inapt*.

incredible or **incredulous**? These two words are sometimes confused. Something that is *incredible* is impossible or difficult to believe (*a frankly incredible story*), whereas someone who is *incredulous* does not or cannot believe what they are told or witnessed (*received my explanation with an incredulous stare*). *Incredible* is also used informally to mean 'amazing' or 'wonderful': *an incredible piece of good luck*.

incredulous or **incredible**? See **incredible** or **incredulous**?

indexes or **indices**? The plural of *index* in its common sense of an alphabetical guide or catalogue is *indexes* (*a book with two indexes*; *card indexes*). In technical uses, especially in mathematics and economics, the plural is more commonly *indices*: *indices of economic progress*.

indices or **indexes**? See **indexes** or **indices**?

inept or **inapt**? See **inapt** or **inept**?

infectious or **contagious**? See **contagious** or **infectious**?

infer or **imply**? See **imply** or **infer**?

inflammable or **flammable**? See **flammable** or **inflammable**?

infringe or **impinge**? See **impinge** or **infringe**?

ingenious or **ingenuous**? These two words are easy to confuse. *Ingenious* means 'clever' or 'effective', especially in an original or surprising way: *an ingenious method of recycling household waste*. *Ingenuous* means 'innocent', 'artless', or 'guileless': *too ingenuous to imagine that they might not mean what they said*.

ingenuous or **ingenious**? See **ingenious** or **ingenuous**?

inhuman or **inhumane**? These are both words of condemnation: *inhuman* is, however, a considerably stronger one than *inhumane*. *Inhumane* means 'lacking compassion or kindness' (*inhumane treatment of animals*). To describe someone's treatment of animals or other people as *inhuman*, however, suggests that it is deliberately cruel or shockingly neglectful and shows none of the qualities that are desirable in a human being: *inhuman torture of prisoners*.

inhumane or **inhuman**? See **inhuman** or **inhumane**?

inquire or **enquire**? See **enquire** or **inquire**?

insurance or **assurance**? See **assurance** or **insurance**?

insure, **ensure**, or **assure**? See **assure**, **ensure**, or **insure**?

intense or **intensive**? These two words, though similar in form and meaning, have different areas of use. *Intense* usually means 'extreme': *intense heat*; *under intense pressure to find a solution*. It can also be used to describe people who are serious and feel emotion deeply (*a very intense young man*) and, when used in connection with people and their activities, usually suggests a high degree of personal commitment or emotional involvement: *an intense effort to stave off bankruptcy*. *Intensive*, on the other hand, is used more objectively and means 'highly concentrated', suggesting organized effort more than personal involvement: *intensive farming*; *conducted an intensive search of the area*.

intensive or **intense**? See **intense** or **intensive**?

inter-, **intra-**, or **intro-**? These three prefixes are easily confused. *Inter-* means 'between': *international*; *intermarriage*. *Intra-* means 'within': *an intrauterine device*. *Intergalactic* travel would go from one galaxy to another; *intragalactic* travel would take place within a single galaxy. *Intro-* means 'inwards': *introspection; an introvert*. The *Internet* is the system of (or between) computer networks throughout the world; an *intranet* is an internal network of computer communications within an organization.

interment or **internment**? These two words are sometimes confused. *Interment* is a formal word for 'burial'; *internment* is the confinement of people who have not committed a crime but are thought to constitute a possible danger to the state, especially in wartime.

internment or **interment**? See **interment** or **internment**?

intra-, **inter-**, or **intro-**? See **inter-**, **intra-**, or **intro-**?

intro-, **intra-**, or **inter-**? See **inter-**, **intra-**, or **intro-**?

Inuit or **Eskimo**? The indigenous peoples of the Arctic prefer to be known as the *Inuit* rather than *Eskimos*. The term *Eskimo* is still sometimes used, but *Inuit* should be preferred.

inveigh or **inveigle**? These two words are sometimes confused. *Inveigh* is always followed by the preposition *against*. To *inveigh against* someone or something is to speak or write about them in a very bitter, hostile, and condemnatory way: *inveighed against the enemies of the working class*. *Inveigle* is followed by a direct object and means 'to use cunning or deceitful methods in order to get someone to do something': *inveigled her into parting with most of her savings*.

inveigle or **inveigh**? See **inveigh** or **inveigle**?

irregardless *Irregardless* is a non-standard word that means 'regardless'. It was probably formed from joining *irrespective* and *regardless*.

irrupt or **erupt**? See **erupt** or **irrupt**?

-ise or **-ize**? Either spelling is correct, in British English, for most of the many verbs, old and new, that end with this suffix: *criticise* or *criticize; privatize* or *privatise*. The *-ize* form reflects the original Greek spelling *-ize*, whereas the *-ise* form reflects an intermediate spelling in French, from which many of these words are derived. Many British people, British newspapers, and British English spellcheckers prefer the *-ise* form. The *-ize* form is, however, standard in American English and totally acceptable in British English, so that it has come to be regarded as the world English norm and, as such, has been adopted by most modern dictionaries and many British publishers. There are, however, a number of verbs which in their standard world English form must end in *-ise*, either because they are related to other words with an *-ise* spelling (such as *advertisement*) or because the ending is not the active suffix *-ize/ise* at all but a longer element such as *-cise* (typically meaning 'cut') or *-vise* (typically meaning 'see'): for example, *advertise, advise, chastise, comprise, compromise, despise, devise, enfranchise, excise, exercise, franchise, improvise, merchandise, revise, supervise, surmise, surprise,* and *televise*.

its or **it's**? Note the difference between these two forms. *Its* is the possessive form of *it* (*The bottle has lost its top; my car is in for its MOT*): it has no apostrophe *s*, but neither has *his* or *ours*. *It's* is a shortened form of *it is* or *it has*: *it's raining; it's been an awful day*. See also pp. 198–200.

-ize or **-ise**? See **-ise** or **-ize**?

jibe, **gibe**, or **gybe**? See **gibe**, **gybe**, or **jibe**?

judgement or **judgment**? Either spelling is acceptable in all varieties of English. In British English, however, *judgement* is often used (with *judgment* in legal contexts), whereas in American English *judgment* is employed in all contexts.

judgment or **judgement**? See **judgement** or **judgment**?

judicial or **judicious**? These two words are sometimes confused. A *judicial* decision is one made by a court of law or by a judge; a *judicious* decision is one that shows wisdom and good judgment. A person can be described as *judicious* but not as *judicial*. *Judicial* is typically used in phrases such as *a judicial enquiry*, *judicial proceedings*, and *the British judicial system*.

judicious or **judicial**? See **judicial** or **judicious**?

junction or **juncture**? A *junction* is a place at which two or more things join (*a road junction*; *a junction box*). *Juncture* is a fairly formal word meaning 'a point in time' especially one at which important developments are taking place: *at this critical juncture the USA decided to intervene*. *At this juncture* is sometimes used to mean simply 'at this moment' or 'now'. This is a cliché and should be avoided.

juncture or **junction**? See **junction** or **juncture**?

kind, **sort**, and **type** Though quite common in casual speech, constructions such as *these kind of things*, *those type of people* are ungrammatical and should be avoided in careful speech or writing. *This sort of thing* is a perfectly acceptable phrase; problems arise when a plural form is required because the singular form does not seem inclusive enough. *These sorts of thing* or *those* *types of books* are grammatically correct. Understood strictly, however, these phrases imply that there are several different categories of thing or book involved. Probably the best and most elegant way of overcoming the difficulty is to reverse the construction: *books of that kind* (many books, all of the same type) or *books of those kinds* (many books of several different types).

latter and **former** See **former** and **latter**.

lay or **lie**? These two words are sometimes confused, especially since the past tense of *lie* is *lay*. To *lay* (past tense *laid*, past participle *laid*) usually takes a direct object and describes the action of putting something down: *to lay a carpet; to lay an egg; she laid herself down on the bed*. To *lie* (past tense *lay*, past participle *lain*) never takes a direct object and describes the state of resting on something: *I think better lying down; he lay groaning on the sofa; the stones had lain undisturbed for centuries*. To *lie* meaning 'to tell untruths' is a completely separate verb – its past tense and past participle is *lied*.

learn *Learn* should never be used to mean 'teach'. *Learn* never takes a personal pronoun or a person's name as a direct object: *I learnt my acting skills from her; she taught me to act*.

leave or **let**? There are one or two phrases in which *leave* is often used as a substitute for *let* with the meaning 'allow (someone) to do something', especially *leave alone, leave go*, and *leave be*. These are acceptable in conversational English, but *leave go* and *leave be* should not be used in formal writing. *Leave someone alone* needs special care since it can mean both *let someone alone* (not interfere with them) and, literally, to leave someone on their own. Compare: *If you'd left your little brother alone, he* *wouldn't have hit you* and *How could you just go off and leave your little brother alone?*

lend, **loan**, and **borrow** These words are sometimes confused. To *lend* means 'to allow someone to take and use something that is yours'. It can be followed by a personal pronoun or a person's name as indirect object: *They lent me their lawn mower.* To *borrow* means the opposite: 'to take and use something that belongs to someone else': *I borrowed their lawn mower.* To show who lent you the thing you borrowed, use *from*: *I borrowed ten pounds from Bob.* To *borrow* something *off* someone is only acceptable in very informal English. To *loan* means the same as to *lend* and is mainly used with reference to money: *The bank loaned them £100,000. Loan* is also a noun: *a loan of £10,000; requested the loan of our lawn mower.*

less or **fewer**? See **fewer** or **less**?

lest *Lest* should be followed by a verb in the subjunctive form (pp. 57–9) or by a verb formed with *should*: *lest it rain before we are finished; lest there should be any doubt about the seriousness of the situation.*

let or **leave**? See **leave** or **let**?

liable, **apt**, and **likely** See **apt**, **liable**, and **likely**.

liaison This word is often misspelt. It has two *i*'s and one *a*.

licence or **license**? In British English *licence* is the only spelling for the noun meaning 'freedom of action' or 'a document authorizing the holder to do or possess something': *a licence to kill; May I see your licence, please?* The spelling for the equivalent verb in British and American English is *license*: *You are only licensed* *to drive vehicles in categories C, D, and E.* Thus also *licensed premises* and a *licensed restaurant* – one that has been granted a licence to serve alcoholic drink. In American English, the spelling *license* is used for both the verb and the noun.

license or **licence**? See **licence** or **license**?

lie or **lay**? See **lay** or **lie**?

lightening or **lightning**? See **lightning** or **lightening**?

lightning or **lightening**? The flash in a thunderstorm is *lightning* without an *e*. *Lightening* comes from the verb lighten: if you see a *lightening* in the sky, dawn is about to break or the clouds are about to part.

like and **such as** Sometimes the use of *like* can be ambiguous: *a boy like you* could mean either 'a boy, for example, you' or 'a boy who resembles you'. The ambiguity can be avoided if *like* is used to introduce a comparison and *such as* is used to introduce an example. However, in the latter case, the use of *such as* is normally restricted to more formal contexts.

-like Adjectives ending in *-like* may be written with or without a hyphen (*catlike, hair-like*) although common compound adjectives ending in *-like* are usually written without a hyphen (*child-like, lifelike*). When *-like* is attached to a word ending in *-ll* a hyphen is added (*bell-like*). When the root word ends in a single *l*, the spelling with or without a hyphen is permissible: *owllike* or *owl-like*.

likely *Likely* is not used on its own as an adverb meaning 'probably' in British English. A sentence such as *They will likely try again* is acceptable in American but not in British English. However, phrases such as *quite likely*, *more than likely*, and *very likely* present no problems: *They have very likely been delayed; She will more than likely call again*. See also **apt**, **liable**, and **likely**.

likely, **liable**, and **apt** See **apt**, **liable**, and **likely**.

liqueur or **liquor**? These two words are sometimes confused. A *liqueur* is a particular type of alcoholic drink that is strong, sweet, and usually drunk in small quantities at the end of a meal: *Cointreau and Tia Maria are popular liqueurs. Liquor* is alcoholic drink in general: *He took the pledge in 1995 and hasn't touched a drop of liquor since*.

liquor or **liqueur**? See **liqueur** or **liquor**?

literally *Literally* is commonly used to show that a familiar phrase or idiom is especially relevant or should be understood in a real or physical sense: *He was literally red with anger*. It is also used informally as a kind of intensifier in a metaphor, in which the literal meaning is apparently absurd: *He was literally beside himself with anger*. This last use is justifiable in linguistic terms, but is controversial.

loan See **lend**, **loan**, and **borrow**.

loath, **loth**, or **loathe**? *Loath* and *loth* are alternative spellings of the same word, an adjective meaning 'reluctant': *She was very loath to part with the money. Loath* is the preferred spelling in modern English. *Loathe* is a verb meaning 'to dislike intensely': *I absolutely loathe greasy food*.

loathe, **loath**, or **loth**? See **loath**, **loth**, or **loathe**?

loose or **lose**? The spelling of these two words can cause problems. *Loose*, spelt with *-oo-* and pronounced with a soft *s* to rhyme with *goose*, is mainly used as an adjective meaning 'not tight': *a loose-fitting dress; the knot has worked loose*. *Lose*, with one *o* and pronounced to rhyme with *whose*, is a verb meaning 'to be unable to find': *I'm always losing my spectacles*.

lose or **loose**? See **loose** or **lose**?

loth, loath, or **loathe**? See **loath, loth,** or **loathe**?

lour or **lower**? See **lower** or **lour**?

lower or **lour**? Either spelling is possible for this verb which means 'to look threatening' or 'to frown': *a lowering* or *louring sky full of black clouds*. In this sense they are pronounced to rhyme with 'tower'.

luxuriant or **luxurious**? These two words are sometimes confused. *Luxuriant* means 'growing thickly and abundantly': *luxuriant vegetation*. It can also, less commonly, mean 'highly ornamented': *luxuriant prose*. *Luxurious* is the adjective connected with the ordinary sense of *luxury*: *the sort of luxurious accommodation you would expect from a five-star hotel*.

luxurious or **luxuriant**? See **luxuriant** or **luxurious**?

male or **masculine**? *Male* is used to describe the sex that does not bear offspring, and plants or flowers that do not produce fruit or seeds: *a male deer is called a stag*. *Masculine* is used only of human beings, not plants or animals, and describes qualities and behaviour that are characteristic of or traditionally ascribed to men rather than women. *He doesn't think pink sheets are very masculine*. *Masculine* is also used in some languages to describe nouns, adjectives, and pronouns, in contrast to those that are feminine or neuter.

man *Man* can be used without an indefinite or definite article to mean the human species or the whole human race: *Man is a political animal*. This usage is, however, felt by many people to be inappropriate in the modern age since it suggests that the male defines or embodies the species, ignoring the female. *Man* should not be used unthinkingly in any context to mean 'men and women' or 'the human race'. Substitutes are *humanity, human beings, the human race, humans, humankind, people,* or, occasionally, *individual* or *person: one person, one vote*. Many compounds with 'man' (and 'woman') can be altered to gender-inclusive forms: *man-hours* to *working hours; man-made* to *artificial* or *synthetic; cameraman* and *camerawoman* to *camera operator; fireman* and *firewoman* to *firefighter; policeman* and *policewoman* to *police officer*.

mankind The same objection is often raised to the use of *mankind* to mean 'human beings as a race or species' as to the use of *man* in the same sense: it seems sexist. The expressions *humanity, humankind, human beings,* and *the human race* will generally fit neatly into any context where *mankind* might be employed and should be preferred. See also **man**.

masculine or **male**? See **male** or **masculine**?

masterful or **masterly**? Both these words can be used to mean 'having or showing the skill of a master', but *masterly* should be preferred in this sense: *a masterly performance; a quite masterly exposition of a very difficult topic*. The main sense of *masterful* is 'showing strength or dominance': *a masterful type who took charge in any situation*. In modern usage *masterly* cannot be used in this sense.

masterly or **masterful**? See **masterful** or **masterly**?

may or **can**? See **can** or **may**?

media *Media* is a plural form, the plural of *medium*: *Television is a medium*; *Television and radio are media*. The form *a media* is grammatically incorrect. The form *the media* meaning 'all the various institutions that spread news and information' should be followed by a plural verb: *The media have shown little interest in this event*. '*He looks forward to an age where the media is redundant*' (*The Guardian*) is incorrect. It is perfectly acceptable usage to use *media* in front of another noun: *a media event*.

meter or **metre**? In British English a *metre* is a measurement of length equal to 100 centimetres, while a measuring instrument is a *meter*: *to read the meter*. Likewise, in British English, the rhythmic pattern of a line of poetry is its *metre*, though the words for specific types of *metre* end in *-er*: *hexameter*; *iambic pentameter*. In American English the spelling *meter* is used for all these senses.

metre or **meter**? See **meter** or **metre**?

militate or **mitigate**? These two words are sometimes confused. *Militate* is related in form and meaning to *militant* and *military*, and its earliest meaning is 'to serve as a soldier' or 'to fight'. It is usually followed by *against* and in modern English means 'to exert a powerful influence against' or 'to make very difficult or unlikely': *Present circumstances militate against an early resumption of peace talks*. *Mitigate* is followed by a direct object and means 'to make less severe': *measures intended to mitigate the harshness of prison life*.

millennium *Millennium* is spelt with two *l*'s and two *n*'s, separated by an *e*.

minuscule *Minuscule* meaning 'tiny' or 'a small letter' is spelt with one *i* and two *u*'s. It can never be spelt *miniscule*.

Miss, Mrs, or **Ms**? See **Ms, Mrs,** or **Miss**?

misuse or **abuse**? See **abuse** or **misuse**?

mitigate or **militate**? See **militate** or **mitigate**?

momentary or **momentous**? *Momentary* means 'lasting only a moment or a very short space of time': *a momentary hesitation; a momentary lapse of concentration*. It should not be confused with *momentous*, which means 'very important' or 'having far-reaching consequences': *a momentous decision; a momentous event*.

momentous or **momentary**? See **momentary** or **momentous**?

moral or **morale**? These two words are sometimes confused. *Moral*, the adjective, with a stress on the first syllable, means 'relating to principles of right and wrong' (*moral judgments*) or 'showing a proper sense of right and wrong' (*a moral person*). As a noun, *moral* usually means 'the moral lesson to be drawn from a story'. *Morale*, with a stress on the second syllable, means 'the general mood of a group of people': *The general decided to lay on a concert party to boost the troops' morale*.

morale or **moral**? See **moral** or **morale**?

Mrs, Ms, or **Miss**? See **Ms, Mrs,** or **Miss**?

Ms, Mrs, or **Miss**? Traditionally, the title *Miss* was used by a woman before marriage together with her maiden name, while *Mrs* was used after marriage together with her husband's surname: *Miss Jones became Mrs Smith when she married*. From the 1950s onwards, the title *Ms* began to be used by women who did not wish to disclose their marital status, thought it irrelevant, or felt that an all-purpose title for women equivalent to *Mr* was needed. This title was also used by some people when writing to or addressing women whose marital status was unknown: it is very useful for this purpose. *Ms* is gradually acquiring wider acceptance, especially among younger people. Some people, however, dislike its associations with feminism and insist on using or being addressed by the traditional titles.

mutual, **reciprocal**, or **common**? These three words are some-times confused. *Mutual* and *reciprocal* can both mean 'directed towards each other'. Two people can be said to share *a mutual* or *reciprocal hatred*, if they hate each other. They can also, how-ever, be said to share *a common hatred* if they both independently hate the same other thing or other person. Because *common* has several other meanings apart from 'shared', *mutual* is sometimes used where the strictly correct word would be *common*. The best-known example is *our mutual friend*, meaning 'your friend as well as mine', a phrase that is now generally acceptable and reinforced by the title of Dickens' novel, whereas *our common friend* might be thought to mean 'our vulgar friend'.

native There are few problems with *native* used as an adjective: *native land*, *native language*, and *native Liverpudlian* are all unexceptionable. It is with the noun that the trouble starts. The word *native* is extremely offensive if used to mean simply 'a non-white person', and scarcely less so now if used to mean 'an original (and by implication usually uncivilized) inhabitant of a country'. The only currently safe use of the noun *native* is in the meaning 'a person who was born in a particular place': *I am a native of Hertfordshire*. See also **Native American**.

Native American This is now generally accepted as the correct term to use for a person whose ancestors lived in America before the arrival of Europeans. The term *Red Indian* for a Native (North) American should be avoided. See also **American Indian**.

naught or **nought**? In British English *nought* is the usual spelling for the word meaning 'o' or 'zero': *a one followed by six noughts*. This word is usually spelt *naught* in American English. In both British English and American English *naught* is a rather literary term meaning 'nothing': *naught for your comfort; come to naught*.

Negro See **black**, **Negro**, and **coloured**.

neither *Neither*, like *either*, should be followed by a verb in the singular when it is the subject of a sentence: *Neither of them was caught*. If two or more particular things or people are being mentioned, *neither* is followed by *nor*, not by *or*: *Neither Janet nor her sister is coming*. If both subjects are singular, a singular verb should be used (*Neither Peter nor Andrew is intending to come*), and if both subjects are plural, a plural verb should be used (*Neither relatives nor friends were made to feel welcome*). Where there is a combination of singular and plural subjects, it is best to let the form of the second one determine the form of the verb: *Neither he nor you are entirely blameless*. See also pp. 11–12.

non or **non-**? *Non* as a prefix is generally used with a hyphen in British English to preserve the identity of the word elements, especially in forms such as *non-event* and *non-native*, and in longer words such as *non-productive* and *non-professional*. In American English, and increasingly in British English, *non-*

words are spelt as single words: *nonstandard*; *nonviolence*. Some words have become familiar as single words, for example *nonconformist* and *nonentity*.

non- and **un-** See **un-** and **non-**.

none *None* can be used with a singular or a plural verb, depending on the meaning. To emphasize the individuals in a group, the singular is used, and *none* is equivalent to 'not one': *None of them is a professional actor*. To emphasize a group or collection of people or things, the plural is more usual and *none* is equivalent to the plural meaning of 'not any': *None of them are professional actors*. A singular construction can often sound formal or pedantic: *None of them is over eighteen*. When *none* is used of non-countable things, it is treated as singular and is equivalent to the singular meaning of 'not any': *None of the cheese is left*.

non-social See **antisocial**, **asocial**, **non-social**, **unsociable** or **unsocial**?

notable or **noticeable**? These two words are close in meaning but there is nevertheless a clear distinction between them. *Notable* means 'worthy of notice' and thus, often, 'important' or 'remarkable': *a notable achievement*. *Noticeable*, on the other hand, means 'visible' or 'perceptible': *a noticeable improvement in quality*. A *notable difference* between two things would generally be a large as well as a significant one, whereas a *noticeable* difference might only be very small.

noticeable or **notable**? See **notable** or **noticeable**?

nought or **naught**? See **naught** or **nought**?

number of The phrase *a number of* meaning 'some' or 'several' should be used with a verb in the plural: *There are a number of things to discuss*; *A number of you, I know, disagree.* When *number* means 'the overall quantity in' *the number of* is used with a singular verb: *The number of meningitis cases is increasing.*

of *Of* should never be spoken, let alone written, following *could, should, would,* or *must.* For example, *I should have told you* can become *I should've told you* in colloquial speech or writing, but *I should of told you* is always wrong.

official or **officious**? A letter, a document, or an announcement can be *official* ('written or made by someone in authority'). Only a person or their words or behaviour can be *officious* in its ordinary meaning. It is an uncomplimentary word meaning 'bossy and interfering'.

officious or **official**? See **official** or **officious**?

older or **elder**? See **elder** or **older**?

one *One* is a useful word for making statements that apply to everyone in general and no one in particular: *One seldom makes that particular mistake twice. You* can serve the same purpose (*You can't make an omelette without breaking eggs*) and sounds less formal and impersonal. It must be clear, however, that *you* is intended to have a general meaning and does not refer to a particular person or particular people. *One* does sound rather formal, but it does not sound too affected unless it is being used in place of *I.*

one another or **each other**? See **each other** or **one another**?

only The notion that the adverb *only* should always be placed next to the word in the sentence that it refers to is a superstition that runs counter to the natural position of such modifying words in English (compare *often* and *usually*). The typical position is between the subject and the verb in sentences such as *I only drink wine at weekends* and after an auxiliary verb in sentences such as *I can only lend you a pound.* (Compare *I often drink wine at weekends* and *I can usually lend you a pound.*) In ordinary conversation, the tone of voice makes it clear that *only* refers forward to the phrase *at weekends* and not more immediately to the words *drink* or *wine*, and that the sense is not (for example) *I drink wine at weekends but I don't cook with it* or *I drink wine at weekends but not beer*. In more formal written English, especially in legal documents, the position of *only* becomes more important, because in these contexts the language needs to be precise. So a contract, for example, might include the words *This penalty will be applied only if the contractor has been warned in writing at least three weeks in advance of the due date*. But in ordinary English *only* would go after the verb *will*.

onto There is no objection to spelling *onto* as a single word when it means 'into a position on': *The book fell onto the floor*. Some people have reservations about using *onto* after a verb that is often followed by the preposition *on*. In a sentence such as *We walked on to the end of the lane* ('until we reached'), *onto* would be incorrect. Compare *We walked onto the end of the red carpet* ('we walked forward and stood on'), in which *onto* is correct. Sentences such as *She latched on to the idea at once* and *I want to move on to another topic* are, however, a grey area. *Onto* is increasingly being used in them, but the safer option is to use *on to*.

or When *or* connects two nouns that are both singular a verb following them must be singular: . . . *if your money or your luggage* *is stolen.* If it connects two plural nouns, the verb is plural: *. . . when your relatives or your friends come to visit.* If *or* separates a singular and a plural noun or two different personal pronouns, the rule is that the verb should agree with whichever comes second: *What if my money or my valuables go missing?; Either you or he has made a mistake.*

oral or **aural**? See **aural** or **oral**?

orient or **orientate**? Both forms of the word are correct. *Orient* is more often used in American English, *orientate* in British English.

orientate or **orient**? See **orient** or **orientate**?

-orous See **-our, -orous**.

ought The negative form of *ought* is *ought not* which can be shortened to *oughtn't*: *Oughtn't we to let them know in advance?* The form *didn't ought* is not standard English. *Ought* should always be connected to a following verb by *to*, even in a sentence such as: *They ought to and could have explained things better.*

-our, -orous Words in British English whose final syllable is spelt *-our*, drop the *u* before the *r* to form adjectives ending in *-ous*: *glamour* but *glamorous*; *humour* but *humorous*. See also p. 157.

out The use of *out* to mean *out of* is standard in American English but seems rather casual in British English and is better avoided in formal writing or speech: *She simply turned and walked out of* (American also *walked out*) *the door.*

overlay or **overlie**? *Overlay*, like *lay*, takes a direct object and refers to an action, the action of putting something on top of something else: *They overlaid the wood with gold leaf. Overlie*, like *lie*, refers to a state, that of being on top of something else: *A thick covering of snow overlies the lawn and flowerbeds. Overlie* has the past tense *overlay*. Note that, unlike *lie*, *overlie* takes a direct object. See also **lay** or **lie**?

overlie or **overlay**? See **overlay** or **overlie**?

owing to or **due to**? See **due to** or **owing to**?

partially or **partly**? These two words are often interchangeable, but there is a subtle distinction between them that is worth noting. *Partly* is the preferable choice with the meaning 'as regards one part': *The building is constructed partly of brick and partly of stone. Partially* is the preferable choice with the meaning 'to a limited extent; incompletely': *partially sighted. Partly* is more common than *partially* to introduce an explanatory clause or phrase, sometimes in the expression *partly . . . partly*: *Partly because of the weather and partly because of the weak economy, profits were down last year.*

partly or **partially**? See **partially** or **partly**?

passed or **past**? These two words, which are pronounced the same, are sometimes confused. *Passed* is the only standard form of the past tense and past participle of *to pass*: *We passed the house on our way to the bus stop; That danger has now passed. Past* is used for all other forms: noun, adjective, preposition, and adverb: *That's all in the past; Past mistakes should be forgotten; half past three; The car drove past.* The possibility of confusion is perhaps greatest in sentences such as: *Time passed very slowly* (because the phrase *time past* is possible: *remembrances of time past*) or *What's past is past* (because *what's past* sounds like a shortened form of *what has passed*). As a rule of thumb, *passed* rarely follows *is* and *past* rarely follows *has*.

past or **passed**? See **passed** or **past**?

people or **persons**? *People* is generally used as the plural of *person*: *one person; two people*. The form *persons* is reserved for formal or legal contexts: *committed by a person or persons unknown*.

perceptible or **perceptive**? *Perceptible* refers to things perceived, *perceptive* to the people perceiving them. *Perceptible* means 'that can be seen, heard or sensed': *a perceptible change in their attitude; The difference is barely perceptible. Perceptive* means 'showing a sharp awareness': *a very perceptive comment; perceptive enough to see that there was something strange going on.*

perceptive or **perceptible**? See **perceptible** or **perceptive**?

perquisite or **prerequisite**? *Perquisite* is the full and formal form of the common word *perk*: the *perquisites of an office* are the additional or fringe benefits someone acquires by being in office over and above the position and the salary. *Prerequisite* is usually followed by the preposition *for* and means 'a necessary condition or attribute': *The presentation of a passport or a birth certificate is a prerequisite for the issuing of a marriage licence.*

persons or **people**? See **people** or **persons**?

phenomena or **phenomenon**? See **phenomenon** or **phenomena**?

phenomenon or **phenomena** *Phenomenon* is a singular noun. *Phenomena* is its plural and should never be used as if it were singular: *a strange phenomenon that occurs during an eclipse; the strange phenomena that occur during eclipses.*

plain or **plane**? These two words, which are pronounced the same, are sometimes confused. *Plain* is usually an adjective and has many adjectival meanings – 'clear', 'ordinary', 'undecorated', 'unattractive', etc.: *That makes everything plain; plain water; a plain Jane.* It has only one common noun sense – 'an area of flat country': *the rolling plains of the American West. Plane,* on the other hand, has many noun senses – 'an aircraft', 'a levelling tool', 'a level': *He's on a different plane to the rest of us.* It has only two adjectival senses: 'completely flat' (*a plane surface*) or 'two-dimensional' (*a plane figure*).

plane or **plain**? See **plain** or **plane**?

politic or **political**? See **political** or **politic**?

political or **politic**? These two words are not interchangeable. *Political* is much the commoner word and means, broadly, 'having to do with politics'. *Politic* means 'sensible or advantageous under the circumstances' and can be used in contexts which have nothing at all to do with politics: *It might be politic to postpone your visit.*

practicable or **practical**? See **practical** or **practicable**?

practical or **practicable**? These two words are close together in meaning and sometimes confused. A *practical* plan or suggestion is one that is useful, realistic, and effective: the *practical* applications of a theory. A *practicable* plan is, simply, one that it is possible to carry out. It might, for instance, be *practicable* to carry a grand piano on the roof of a car, but this is not a very *practical* method of transporting it. A person can be described as *practical* ('good at ordinary tasks' or 'down-to-earth'), but not as *practicable*.

practice or **practise**? In British English *practice* is the correct spelling for the noun in all its senses: *do some piano practice; in theory and in practice; a veterinary practice.* The spelling for the equivalent verb is *practise*: *to practise the piano; to practise one's religion; a practising dental surgeon.* In American English, the spelling *practice* is used for both the noun and the verb.

practise or **practice**? See **practice** or **practise**?

precede or **proceed**? These two words are sometimes confused. To *precede* is to 'go before': *She preceded me into the room; The meeting had been held on the Tuesday preceding the Easter weekend.* To *proceed* means to 'go forward': *I was proceeding along the High Street; The work is proceeding well.* Only *proceed* can be followed by *to* and another verb: *She then proceeded to read the paragraph in question.*

prerequisite or **perquisite**? See **perquisite** or **prerequisite**?

prescribe or **proscribe**? To *prescribe* is what doctors do – they specify a particular medicine for a patient. It means 'to lay down or order' positively that something should be done: *in the form prescribed by law.* To *proscribe* is a much rarer word and it has the opposite meaning – 'to forbid' or 'to ban': *Such practices were considered immoral and were proscribed by law.*

presently The standard British English meaning of *presently* used to be 'soon', 'in a minute': *I'll be with you presently.* What used to be thought of as an American or Scottish meaning 'now', 'at present' or 'currently' (*He's presently engaged with a client*) is becoming increasingly widely used in British English as well. The tense of the verb is usually an indicator of which sense is intended: used with the future tense the meaning is 'soon'; with the present tense the meaning is 'now'. Care should be taken to avoid the ambiguity in a sentence such as: *He's presently starting a new job.*

presume or **assume**? See **assume** or **presume**?

principal or **principle**? These two words, which are pronounced the same, are often confused. *Principle* is only ever a noun and has the basic sense of 'a fundamental truth or standard': *It's the principle of the thing; I object to that on principle. Principal* is most often used as an adjective meaning 'main': *their principal aim in life.* As a noun, *principal* means the 'head of an educational establishment' (it is the American English word for a 'head-teacher') or 'a leading actor or performer'.

principle or **principal**? See **principal** or **principle**?

proceed or **precede**? See **precede** or **proceed**?

program or **programme**? British English has adopted the spelling *program* as standard in computer contexts: *a computer program; to program a computer.* In all other contexts the correct British English spelling is *programme*, while the correct American English spelling is *program*.

programme or **program**? See **program** or **programme**?

proscribe or **prescribe**? See **prescribe** or **proscribe**?

protagonist Strictly speaking, only dramas have *protagonists*. The word, which comes from Greek, originally meant 'first or main actor' and became extended to mean 'the main or a main character' in a drama, an artistic work, or a dramatic real-life situation: *By chapter three the protagonist is in conflict with all the other members of her family. Protagonist* is also frequently used to mean a 'supporter' (*a protagonist of the campaign/movement*). This use is based, it is suggested, on the mistaken assumption that the *pro-* at the beginning of the word is the common prefix meaning 'in favour of', whereas in fact the prefix involved is *prot(o)-* 'first', as in *prototype*. Given that it is based on a mistake and that it often represents an attempt to find a fancy substitute for 'supporter' or 'advocate', this use is best avoided.

questionnaire *Questionnaire* is spelt with two *n*'s and one *r*.

raise or **rise?** *Raise* is a verb with *raised* as the regular past tense and past participle and it takes a direct object: *All those in favour please raise your hands*. *Rise* is a verb with an irregular past tense (*rose*) and past participle (*risen*) and it never takes a direct object: *Leave the dough to rise for at least an hour*. In British English an increase in salary is also called *a rise*, while American English calls it *a raise*.

re- Most verbs that begin with the prefix *re-* meaning 'again' are spelt without a hyphen: *reboot the computer*; *recycle domestic waste*. Some people prefer to use a hyphen when the verb to which *re-* is attached begins with a vowel, especially *e*. However, spellings such as *reinsure* and *reuse* are shown in all modern British English dictionaries and forms such as *reentry* and *reexamine* in some. The hyphen is crucial, however, where two different meanings are involved, for example in distinguishing between *re-cover* ('cover again') and *recover* ('recuperate'), *re-creation* ('creating anew') and *recreation* ('leisure'), or *re-form* ('form again') and *reform* ('change for the better').

reason It is argued by some traditionalists that when *reason* means 'cause' it already contains the idea expressed by causal words such as *because* and *why*, which means that it is unnecessary and incorrect to use them together with it. Strictly then, the sentence *The reason that the plan failed was that it overlooked two simple facts* is correct, and the sentence *The reason why the plan failed was because it overlooked two simple facts* is incorrect. Any problems in sentences involving *reason* can often be regarded by recasting and leaving out the word *reason* altogether: *The plan failed because it overlooked two simple facts.*

reciprocal, **mutual**, or **common**? See **mutual**, **reciprocal**, or **common**?

regretful or **regrettable**? *Regretful* refers to the state of somebody's feelings: *Do you feel at all regretful about missing the opportunity? Regrettable*, on the other hand, comments on an event, an action, or a state of affairs: *It is most regrettable that she didn't see fit to come and answer these questions in person.*

regrettable or **regretful**? See **regretful** or **regrettable**?

replace or **substitute**? These two words are close in meaning but differ somewhat in use. One *replaces* an old thing *with* a new thing, or one *substitutes* a new thing *for* an old thing. The meaning is essentially the same in both cases, but the prepositions are different (*replace . . . with* (or *by*); *substitute . . . for*) and the order in which 'old thing' and 'new thing' follow the verb is also different: *replace the House of Lords with an elected second chamber; substitute an elected second chamber for the House of Lords.*

restive or **restless**? Because they are similar not only in form but also in meaning, these two words are difficult to keep apart. *Restive* means 'difficult to control or keep still': children and horses are commonly described as *restive* and the word is also applied to people who get impatient with restrictions placed on them: *The military were growing restive and kept urging the government to act.* Restless ('fidgety', 'unable to rest', or 'constantly moving') is applied much more widely than *restive* – not only to people, but also to movements and things: *restless pacing to and fro; a restless night.*

restless or **restive**? See **restive** or **restless**?

reverend or **reverent**? *Reverend* is a title used for a member of the clergy: *the Reverend Val Hughes. Reverent* is an adjective meaning 'deeply respectful': *A reverent hush descended on the congregation.*

reverent or **reverend**? See **reverend** or **reverent**?

rise or **raise**? See **raise** or **rise**?

round, **around**, or **about**? See **around**, **round**, or **about**?

salubrious or **salutary**? These two words are sometimes confused. *Salubrious* is a fairly formal word, though often used humorously, meaning 'health-promoting' and thus 'hygienic' or 'decent': *There was a toilet, but it wasn't what you'd call salubrious.* A *salutary* experience or reminder, on the other hand, is one that teaches a necessary and beneficial lesson: *not a pleasant experience, but a very salutary one.*

salutary or **salubrious**? See **salubrious** or **salutary**?

same The use of *same* as a pronoun (*To installing one electric shower and connecting and testing same: £170*) is a commercial or legal use. It should not be used in formal speech or writing.

Scotch, **Scots**, or **Scottish**? *Scotch* is, for general purposes, an outdated adjective and disliked by many Scots. It should only be used in the specific combinations where it is familiar and established: *a Scotch egg; Scotch whisky*. *Scottish* is an all-purpose adjective that can be used for people, places, and things in or relating to Scotland: *a Scottish soldier; a Scottish tourist resort; the Scottish education system*. *Scots* may be used to describe people (*a Scots politician, the Scots Guards*), but its use seems to be becoming less common.

Scots, Scotch, or **Scottish**? See **Scotch, Scots**, or **Scottish**?

Scottish, Scots, or **Scotch**? See **Scotch, Scots**, or **Scottish**?

seasonable or **seasonal**? See **seasonal** or **seasonable**?

seasonal or **seasonable**? These two words are sometimes confused. *Seasonal* means 'connected with or dependent on the season': fruit is naturally *seasonal*, employment in a seaside resort is often *seasonal* and there may be *seasonal* fluctuations in the prices of goods. *Seasonable* is the word that means 'appropriate to the season'. Weather, particularly, can be *seasonable* or *unseasonable*. *Seasonable advice*, therefore, is advice that is given at an appropriate time.

seeing It is permissible in modern English to use *seeing* as a conjunction meaning 'since' or 'in view of the fact that': *Seeing we're late anyway, another five minutes probably won't make any difference*. The correct way to use it, however, is on its own or followed by *that*. The form *seeing as how* is considered non-standard by most modern authorities. Care should also be taken to ensure that the conjunction *seeing* cannot be confused with the present participle of *to see*. *Seeing that he was in trouble, she decided to help him* is ambiguous to the extent that it is not entirely clear whether or not she was an eyewitness to the fact that he was in trouble.

sensual or **sensuous**? *Sensual* is the more common word and the one that frequently carries overtones of sexual desire or pleasure: *pouting sensual lips; sensual pleasures. Sensuous* is the more neutral word: it also means 'appealing to the senses' but without the feeling of self-indulgence or sexiness associated with *sensual: the artist's sensuous use of colour and texture.*

sensuous or **sensual**? See **sensual** or **sensuous**?

separate *Separate* is spelt with two *a*'s and only two *e*'s. It may help to remember that it is related etymologically to the words *pare* and *prepare*.

serial or **cereal**? See **cereal** or **serial**?

sex and **gender** See **gender** and **sex**.

shall or **will**? Traditionally *shall* was used to form the future tense for the first person singular and plural (*I/we shall go tomorrow*) and to state a firm intention if used with any other personal pronoun (*You shall go to the ball; Britons never, never, never shall be slaves*). Conversely *will* formed the future tense for the second and third person (*You/they will know soon enough*) and expressed a firm intention if used with *I* or *we* (*I will not put up with this*). This distinction has largely died out, with *I will* or *we will* being used in informal usage and the general use of the contraction *'ll*, e.g. *I'll, we'll. Shall*, however, is needed when asking questions that relate to the immediate situation: *Shall we dance?* is an invitation to someone to dance now; *Will we dance?* only makes sense if the speaker is looking ahead to the possibility of dancing at some future event, as in *Will there be dancing?*

shear or **sheer**? To *shear* is a verb meaning 'to cut' or 'to be cut': *to shear a sheep; The end of the bolt sheared off*. It has two possible past participles. In the context of cutting hair or wool, or in the figurative meaning 'deprived', the past participle is *shorn*: *a shorn lamb*; *shorn of his authority*. In the context of cutting metal, the past participle is *sheared*: *It had sheared right through the cable*. A pair of *shears* is a cutting implement for garden use. *Sheer* is an adjective, an adverb, and a verb. As an adjective it means 'vertical' (*a sheer cliff*), 'see-through' (*sheer tights*), or 'pure' (*sheer nonsense*; *sheer determination*). As an adverb it means 'straight up or down without a break' (*the cliffs fell sheer*). As a verb, to *sheer*, is 'to swerve' or 'to turn abruptly': *The yacht sheered off at the last moment, narrowly missing the end of the jetty*.

sheer or **shear**? See **shear** or **sheer**?

should or **would**? Traditionally, *should* and *would* were used in reported speech in the same way as *shall* and *will* were used in direct speech – *should* for the first person singular and plural, *would* for the second and third persons: *I said I should be there*; *She told me she would be there*. This distinction is now made more rarely, and *would* is generally used instead of *should*. In spoken and informal contexts any distinction between *should* and *would* is hidden by the use of the contraction *'d*: *I'd*; *we'd*, etc. Note however that only *should* is used with the meaning 'ought to' as in: *I should go, but I don't particularly want to*. See also **shall** or **will**?

sic *Sic* is used when quoting someone else's words exactly to show that a mistake or oddity in them comes from the person quoted, not from the person quoting: *According to the chairman, 'These figures apply only to the months of Febuary (sic) and March.'*

sociable or **social**? See **social** or **sociable**?

social or **sociable**? *Social*, as an adjective, is an all-purpose neutral word meaning 'connected with society': *social conditions; social work*. *Sociable* is a complimentary term used mainly to describe people meaning 'fond of company' or 'friendly': *She's not feeling very sociable this evening*.

sooner When the phrase *no sooner* starts a sentence, the normal order of the verb and subject following it should be reversed: *No sooner had she said this, than the telephone rang*. Note that the correct word to use after *no sooner* is *than*, not *when*: *I had no sooner sat down than Mary started calling for me from the garden*.

sort See **kind, sort,** and **type**.

speciality or **specialty**? The subject that a person specializes in is their *speciality* in British English, but *specialty* in American English.

specially or **especially**? See **especially** or **specially**?

specialty or **speciality**? See **speciality** or **specialty**?

stationary or **stationery**? These two words, which are pronounced the same, are often confused. *Stationary* is the adjective meaning 'standing still': *a stationary vehicle*. *Stationery* refers to the type of goods sold by a *stationer* (which is perhaps the easiest way of remembering the difference in spelling): paper, envelopes and the like.

stationery or **stationary**? See **stationary** or **stationery**?

stimulant or **stimulus**? A *stimulus* (plural *stimuli*) is anything that stimulates a reaction from someone or something: a prod with a stick, a promise of more pay or the threat of dismissal might act as a *stimulus* to somebody, making them work harder.

A *stimulant*, on the other hand, is specifically a substance, especially a drink or drug, that temporarily makes someone more energetic or alert.

stimulus or **stimulant**? See **stimulant** or **stimulus**?

substitute or **replace**? See **replace** or **substitute**?

such as and **like** See **like** and **such as**.

suit or **suite**? Both these words mean a 'set' of things, but different things are involved. A *suit* is a set of clothes or armour, or one of the four sets of playing cards making up a pack (hearts, clubs, spades, or diamonds): *follow suit. Suit* can also mean 'a court action' or 'a request or appeal to someone': *grant somebody's suit.* A *suite* is a set of matching furniture, of rooms, of related pieces of music (*Holst's Planets Suite*), or computer software. It can also mean the retinue of servants or staff attending a grandee or high-ranking official.

suite or **suit**? See **suit** or **suite**?

supersede *Supersede* has no *c* in it and no double *e*. It comes from a Latin verb *supersedēre*, which literally means 'to sit above someone'.

than *My sister can run faster than I.* This is the grammatically correct form – *than I*, as traditionalists frequently point out, is short for *than I can.* However, the form that is considered correct by traditionalists sometimes sounds rather pedantic in speech: *My sister can run faster than I can* is correct, but *My sister can run faster than me* is more frequently used. Filling in the missing verb is often a good way of preserving grammar and avoiding awkwardness: *She spent far less time on it than he did.* It is also important to be aware of the possibility of confusion in a sentence such as: *You know her better than me*. Grammatically, this means 'you know her better than you know me'. It is often used, however, to mean 'you know her better than I do'. This last form of words is the one to adopt to make that particular meaning crystal clear.

thankfully *Thankfully* has now, like *hopefully*, been widely accepted as an adverb that can relate to a whole sentence as well as to a single verb: *Thankfully, no damage was done*. It is usually easy to distinguish in speech between this sense, meaning 'fortunately', and the other sense 'in a thankful way': *He sank down thankfully into the soft warm bed*. In writing, care should be taken to make sure that it is clear which sense is intended.

that, **which**, and **who** The general rule is that either *that* or *which* can be used to introduce clauses attached to nouns that add crucial identifying pieces of information: *The briefcase that* (or *which*) *I left on the train contained important papers* (my other briefcase didn't); *This is the book that* (or *which*) *you need*. There is an increasing tendency for *that* to be preferred to *which* in such sentences, and whichever is used the clause is not separated from the noun by commas. *Which*, on the other hand, must be used in clauses that give purely incidental information: *The weather, which was sunny that day, contributed greatly to the success of the event*. Such clauses must be enclosed by commas and – the crucial test for distinguishing between the two kinds – can be wholly removed from the sentence without making it unclear what is being referred to.

Although *who* is the usual pronoun used for people, it is perfectly acceptable to use *that* in place of it: *I've been sent a letter by someone that I met on holiday; You are the only person that knows the whole truth.* See also pp. 24–6.

their, **there**, or **they're**? These three words, which are pronounced the same, are sometimes confused. *Their* is the possessive form of *they* (*It's their fault; They'll bring their own tools*). *There* is an adverb of place (*You'll find it over there*) and is used with the verb *to be* (*There is nothing I can do about it; Are there any more questions?*). *They're* is the shortened form of *they are*: *They're not quite ready yet.*

themselves and **themself** *Themselves* is the standard reflexive form of *they*: *I hope the children enjoyed themselves. Themself* is a fourteenth- to sixteenth-century form that has recently been revived for use as an equivalent to *they* meaning 'a person of either sex': *No one should blame themself for this tragedy.* There is a certain logic to this if *they* is given a singular meaning, but the form *themselves* is also used in this context: *Everyone ought to try it for themselves.* '*We are looking for a Producer/Director who, when necessary, can use a camera themselves, and who has . . .*' (BBC advertisement). This is a very controversial area of English usage where, in formal writing, it is often best to abide by what is universally approved or to take avoiding action: *Everyone ought to try it for himself or herself* or *Everyone ought to try it personally.* See also **they**.

there, **their**, or **they're**? See **their**, **there**, or **they're**?

they The use of *they* as a singular pronoun meaning 'a person of either sex' has a very long history. It is no less controversial for all that. It is no longer appropriate to use *he, him, his,* or *himself* after words like *everyone* or *no one.* A sentence such as *Everyone should do his best* would rightly be seen as sexist except where all the people referred to were male. The forms *he or she*, *his or her*, etc. are undoubtedly often awkward to use. The use of *they*, *them*, and *their* presents itself as an obvious and convenient solution – except that, traditionally, *they* is plural. A blanket objection to a singular *they* seems unreasonable. It is best perhaps to avoid it in formal writing and where the clash between singular and plural is very marked. *Everyone should do their best* is acceptable inasmuch as *everyone* is a plural concept if not a plural word. *A lawyer must respect their clients' confidence* is far less acceptable and could so easily be recast in unexceptionable form: *Lawyers must respect their clients' confidence*.

they're, **their**, or **there**? See **their**, **there**, or **they're**?

till or **until**? *Till* and *until* can be used interchangeably. *Until* is slightly more formal than *till* and in writing *until* is more commonly found than *till*.

titillate or **titivate**? These two words are sometimes confused. To *titillate* someone means to 'arouse or stimulate someone, especially sexually': *The pictures were mildly titillating, but scarcely obscene*. To *titivate* something is to 'smarten it up': *She couldn't afford a new hat, so she titivated the old one with a new band and a few feathers*.

titivate or **titillate**? See **titillate** or **titivate**?

to, **too**, or **two**? Being pronounced the same, these three words are sometimes confused. *To* is mainly used as a preposition (*to London*; *to the top of the hill*; *to the utmost*) and in forming the infinitive of a verb (*to make*). *Too* is the adverb that means 'overmuch' and usually precedes an adjective (*too difficult for* *me; too hot to handle*). It also means 'as well', in which case it often comes at the end of a sentence (*Can Jenny come too?*). *Two* is the number between one and three (*Two and two make four*).

too, **to**, or **two**? See **to**, **too**, or **two**?

transpire *Transpire* has two common non-technical meanings – 'to become known' (*It eventually transpired that the documents had been lost*) and 'to happen' (*A most unfortunate incident transpired as the guests were leaving the hotel*). The use of the word in the second meaning is objected to by some traditionalists. There are no historical grounds for this, but it is argued, first, that *transpire* is simply a pompous alternative for *happen* or *occur* and, second, that in phrases such as *what transpired at the meeting* it is impossible to know which sense is intended. On these grounds, *transpire* is better avoided in the second sense.

troop or **troupe**? These two words are sometimes confused. A *troop* is a group of soldiers or Scouts, and the word is sometimes extended to mean simply any 'large group': *The visitors were beginning to arrive in troops*. *Troop* can also be used as a verb meaning 'to move in a group': *After the picnic, we trooped back down the hill*. A *troupe* is a group of actors or circus performers.

troupe or **troop**? See **troop** or **troupe**?

turbid or **turgid**? *Turbid* is a comparatively rare, literary word meaning 'muddy' – like a river that is clouded with sediment – or 'confused and obscure'. *Turgid* literally means 'swollen'. It is used most commonly in its extended sense of 'pompous and boring' as an uncomplimentary description of someone's writing style.

turgid or **turbid**? See **turbid** or **turgid**?

two, **too**, or **to**? See **to**, **too**, or **two**?

type See **kind**, **sort**, and **type**.

un- and **non-** Both these prefixes are used to produce negative forms of words. In cases where they can both be attached to the same root, the resulting *un-* word is generally stronger than the *non-* word. A *non-professional* tutor is one who is not qualified; *unprofessional* behaviour contravenes professional ethics. If someone's methods are described as *unscientific*, a criticism is usually implied (the methods do not come up to the standards required by science); if they are described as *non-scientific*, the effect is usually more neutral (the methods come from some field other than science).

underlay or **underlie**? *Underlay* is most commonly a noun meaning a layer of material placed beneath a carpet. When used as a verb *underlay*, like *lay*, takes a direct object and refers to an action, the action of laying something beneath something else: *We underlaid the carpet with felt. Underlie*, like *lie*, refers to a state, that of being underneath something else; but unlike *lie*, *underlie* takes a direct object. It is most commonly used figuratively to mean 'form the basis for': *the underlying causes of the revolution. Underlie* has the past tense *underlay*. See also **lay** or **lie**?

underlie or **underlay**? See **underlay** or **underlie**?

unexceptionable or **unexceptional**? See **unexceptional** or **unexceptionable**?

unexceptional or **unexceptionable**? These two words are quite close together in meaning and could be confused. *Unexceptional* means 'not outstanding', therefore 'ordinary' or 'rather dull' (*an unexceptional year for wine*). If a thing is *unexceptionable* it causes no offence or controversy: *It was just that one remark – the rest of the speech was totally unexceptionable.* See also **exceptional** or **exceptionable**?

uninterested or **disinterested**? See **disinterested** or **uninterested**?

unique If something is *unique* it is the only one of its kind. It is consequently illogical to speak of one thing being *more* or *less unique* than another or of something as being *rather, very, comparatively* or *somewhat unique.* It is correct to talk of, for example, *a unique opportunity* or to describe something as *almost unique* or *nearly unique,* but, where any kind of comparison is implied, it is better to choose another adjective such as *unusual* or *rare.*

unsociable See **antisocial, asocial, non-social, unsociable,** or **unsocial**?

unsocial See **antisocial, asocial, non-social, unsociable,** or **unsocial**?

until or **till**? See **till** or **until**?

used to The strictly correct negative form of *used to* is *used not to,* which can be shortened to *usedn't to*: *You used not to* (or *usedn't to*) *mind if we came in a little late.* This often sounds rather formal, so that *did not use to* or *didn't use to* (but not *didn't used to*) are generally acceptable in informal speech or writing. Likewise, the traditionally correct negative question form *used you not to . . . ?* or *usedn't you to . . . ?* is often replaced, more informally, by *didn't you use to . . . ?* If neither of these options seems acceptable, *you used to . . . , didn't you?* can be used.

venal or **venial**? See **venial** or **venal**?

venial or **venal**? These two words are sometimes confused. *Venial* is usually applied to sins, faults, or errors and means that they are minor and can be forgiven. *Venal* is usually applied to people and means that they can be corrupted or bribed.

waiver or **waver**? See **waver** or **waiver**?

waver or **waiver**? These two words are easily confused. To *waver* is a verb meaning 'to be unable to decide', 'to show signs of indecision', or 'to totter': *A week ago she was firmly on our side, but now she's starting to waver. Waiver* is a noun from the verb to *waive* and means 'a statement or document renouncing a right or claim': *We had to sign a waiver giving up our right to compensation in case of injury.*

well- Adjectives such as *well-mannered* and *well-known* should always be spelt with a hyphen when used before a noun: *a well-mannered young man*; *a well-known story*. The hyphen is not usually necessary when the adjective is used after a verb: *She seemed so well mannered*; *As is probably well known to most of you* . . . The correct way of forming the comparative and superlative of most such adjectives is with *better* and *best*: *the best-equipped research department*; *You would be better advised to wait.*

whether and **if** See **if** and **whether**.

which See **that**, **which**, and **who**.

white When describing people of a particular skin colour, *white*, like black, should generally be used without an initial capital letter. Although *white* is an acceptable term in most contexts, American usage often prefers to refer to race in terms of geographical origin, thus preferring *European* or *Caucasian* to *white*.

Neither of these terms, however, is particularly common British English.

who or **whom**? Grammatically, *who* and *whom* are the subject and object forms respectively of the same word. *Who* corresponds to *I*, *he*, *she*, or *they*; *whom* corresponds to *me*, *him*, *her*, or *them*: *They saw whom? – They saw him*. *Whom*, however, is being increasingly relegated to very formal use in modern English, especially in questions: *Whom have I the honour of addressing?*, but *Who were you speaking to just then?* or *Who did you see at the meeting?* The same is largely true for the use of *whom* as a relative pronoun. Many people would argue that if *the man who I saw yesterday* is grammatically incorrect, *the man whom I saw yesterday* sounds pedantic, and it is better to say *the man that I saw yesterday* or, simply, *the man I saw yesterday*. It is most difficult to avoid *whom* immediately after a preposition: *To whom* (never *to who*) *were you speaking?*; *Nobody told me from whom* (never *from who*) *the message had come*. If the preposition is sent to the end of such sentences, however, the use of *who* seems more acceptable: *Nobody told me who the message had come from* (better still: *who had sent the message*). See also **that**, **which**, and **who**.

whom or **who**? See **who** or **whom**?

who's or **whose**? These two words are pronounced the same, but it is important to distinguish between them in writing, especially in questions. *Who's* is the shortened form of *who is* or *who has*: *Who's that? – It's only me*; *Who's done the washing-up? Whose* is the possessive form of *who*: *Whose is that?* ('Who owns that?'); *Whose turn is it to do the washing-up?* See also pp. 198–200.

whose or **who's**? See **who's** or **whose**?

will or **shall**? See **shall** or **will**?

-wise Sentences such as *How are things going workwise?* and *Careerwise, it seems like a good move* are very commonly used. The use of *-wise* added to the end of a noun, disliked by some traditionalists, is often a neat way of conveying the idea 'as far as something is concerned'. It is not, however, recommended in formal writing, and if *-wise* words are overused, or if *-wise* is attached to a long word or phrase (*research-and-development-wise*; *cost-effectivenesswise*) the results sound like jargon or are unintentionally comic.

worthwhile In front of a noun, *worthwhile* is usually written as one word: (*a worthwhile effort*). After a verb it may be written as either one or two words: *The effort was not worthwhile* (or *worth while*). The two parts of the word are separated in the phrase *to be worth one's while*: *It wouldn't be worth your while to spend too much time on the job.*

would or **should**? See **should** or **would**?

you or **you're**? *Your* is the possessive form of *you* (*It's your turn now; May I borrow your pen?*) and should not be confused with *you're*, which is pronounced the same, but is the shortened form of *you are*: *You're not as young as you were; I hope you're not getting bored.*

you're or **your**? See **your** or **you're**?

3   Spelling

Introduction

English spelling is notoriously difficult and inconsistent. Other languages have what is known as **phonetic spelling**, in which a word is, roughly speaking, spelt as it sounds, each letter of the alphabet corresponding to one particular sound made by the voice. While many of the simpler words in English (*fat*, *cat*, *mat*, etc.) function in this way, most of the more complex ones do not. The number of possible ways in which the combination of letters *-ough*, to take only one particularly strange example, can be pronounced illustrates how far English has moved away from phonetic spelling (compare *cough*, *dough*, *rough*, *slough* and *thorough* – and there are more!). There are rules governing the way words are spelt, which will be set out later in this chapter, and rules can be learnt. People who are not gifted with superb powers of memory or who do not have a natural talent for spelling, however, are still likely to make mistakes. Even with the benefit of the spellcheckers that are incorporated into almost all modern computers and word processors, official and business letters still arrive with spelling mistakes in them. The spelling (and grammar) of many websites on the Internet is notoriously bad. Spelling mistakes are often hard to spot when you are writing and yet somehow so conspicuous when read later.

Putting aside authorial impersonality for a moment, the writers confess to being far from perfect spellers. We trust in the effectiveness of a spellchecker and the eagle eyes of other editors, proofreaders, etc., and hope to provide an unblemished text. Writing with a pen on paper (especially in a hurry) or typing without the benefit of an automatic error-indicator, it is a somewhat different story. The best and perhaps only guard, apart from mechanical aids, against making mistakes is knowledge of your own weak points and reference to a dictionary in cases of doubt. How many *r*'s in *embarrass*, how many *n*'s in *millennium*? If you have difficulties remembering such spellings as these, at least try mentally to flag these words as dangerous. There are dictionaries available that are specifically designed to show the spellings of words (also often indicating the correct places to make syllable breaks if you should need to hyphenate a word to make it fit a line) and including a very brief definition. However, a dictionary cannot help unless it is consulted, that is, unless the writer is aware that they need help.

Sounds and spellings

While it is true to say that English spelling is not particularly phonetic, there is generally a link between the way a word is pronounced and the way it is spelt. Different sounds are reproduced by different combinations of letters. This is most crucial – and most difficult – with regard to vowel sounds. The nature of a vowel also often affects other aspects of spelling such as the dropping or retaining of a final *e* or the doubling of a final consonant.

There are, of course, five vowels in the English alphabet *a, e, i, o, u.* All the other letters are consonants, though *w* and *y* are sometimes referred to as semivowels because they share some of the characteristics of true vowels.

The English language, however, uses rather more vowel sounds than it has letters for and this where the complications arise. Vowel sounds can be pronounced short or long. The vowels in the words *bat, bet, bit, cot, put,* and *but* are all short. The vowels in *father, be,* and *to* are long. Short vowel sounds are usually represented by a single letter – though the short *e* in *bed* is sometimes represented by *ea* (*head, lead* (the metal)). Long vowel sounds can be represented in a number of ways. The *a* sound in *father,* for example, can also be represented by *ar* (*arm*); the *e* in *be* often appears as *ee* (*bee*), *ea* (*bean*), *ei* (*ceiling*), or *ie* (*niece*); while the *o* in *to* may be rendered as *oo* (*too*), *ew* (*flew*), *u* (*flute*), or by *ue* (*blue*).

English is also rich in sounds known as **diphthongs**, combinations of two vowel sounds. If the list of long vowel sounds above seems rather short, this is because many of the long sounds in English are actually diphthongs – for example the *a* sound in *hay* or *rain,* the *i* sound in *lie* or *my,* the *o* sound in *note* or *coat.* The *u* sound in *unit* and *you* is also a combined sound, tacking a *y* onto the long *o* sound.

Spelling rules for vowels: 'i' before 'e'

This chapter gives some of the basic rules of English spelling. One of the easiest spelling rules to remember concerning vowels is one that is – or used to be – taught to every child at primary school: *i before e except after c.* The rule applies to most words in which *ie* represents the long *e* sound: *achieve, believe, brief, chief, diesel, field, grief, hygiene, niece, piece, relieve, reprieve, shield, shriek, siege, thief, wield, yield.* The exception is after *c*: *ceiling, conceit, conceive, deceit, deceive, perceive, receipt, receive*. Exceptions to the general rule include: *caffeine, Keith, Neil, protein, seize, Sheila, species, weir, weird*. And note that the spelling *ei* is used when the sound is *ay*: *beige, deign, eight, freight, neighbour, reign, rein, veil, vein, weigh*.

'y' and 'ie'

The combination *ie* also figures in another useful rule of spelling. Words that end in a consonant followed by *-y* change the *y* to *ie* in order to form most of their inflections (the plural if they are nouns, the comparative and superlative if they are adjectives, and the third person singular of the present tense and past tense and past participle if they are verbs). So, when *fancy* is a noun, its plural is *fancies*; when it is an adjective, its comparative is *fancier* and its superlative is *fanciest*; and when it is a verb we say *he fancies* and *he fancied* (but *fancying*). To give further examples: the plural of *charity* is *charities*; *happy* converts to *happier* and *happiest*; *to vary* makes *he varies, she has varied* (but *varying*).

Words that end with a vowel followed by a *y* do not do this. For the most part they inflect in the normal way. The plural of *boy* is *boys* and of *holiday* is *holidays*; *coy* converts to *coyer* and *coyest*; *annoy* makes *annoys, annoyed*, and *annoying*. The most notable exceptions to this rule are irregular verbs such as *lay, pay*, and *say*, which use *id* to form their past tense and past participle (*laid, paid, said*).

'-os' and '-oes'

Words that end with a combination of a consonant and *o* generally form their plural by adding *-es* (*potato – potatoes; tomato – tomatoes; echo – echoes*). The same applies to the formation of the third person singular of the present tense of verbs that end in a consonant + *o* (*embargo* – *embargoes*). When a word ends in a vowel followed by *o*, it simply adds an *s* (*cameo* – *cameos*, *studio* – *studios*).

Some words add *-es* or *-s* for the plural: *banjo* – *banjos* or *banjoes*; *cargo* – *cargos* or *cargoes*; *ghetto* – *ghettos* or *ghettoes*; *volcano* – *volcanos* or *volcanoes*; *zero* – *zeros* or *zeroes*. At least the original rule covers *potato* and *tomato* and you would not go wrong in following it for all the words that have alternative plurals!

Dropping or retaining '-e'

English words that contain a long vowel or diphthong often end with a silent *-e*: *hate, invite, nice, note, cute*. When these words are nouns and adjectives they cause few problems – they add *s* to form the plural in the normal way (*hates, notes*) and form the comparative and superlative by adding *-r* and *-st* (*nicer, nicest; cuter, cutest*). Another, and more accurate, way of putting that last point would be to say that they drop their own silent *e* and add the standard suffixes *-er* and *-est*. The distinction is quite important because the rule of spelling that concerns these words is usually formulated like this. Words that end in a silent *e* drop it in order to add a suffix that begins with a vowel.

To give some examples. The verb *to note* has the present participle (*-ing* form) *noting* and the past participle *noted*. The *e* is dropped to make the adjective *notable* because the suffix *-able* begins with a vowel. Following the same pattern, from *bore* we get *boring*, from *hope* we get *hoping*, from *precise* comes *precision*. There are a few exceptions where the *e* is not omitted before *-ing*. For example *singeing* ('scorching') to differentiate it from *singing* a song; *routeing* ('arranging a route') to differentiate it from *routing* ('defeating decisively'). There is a growing tendency to omit the *-e* before the suffixes *-able* and *-age*: *lovable* or *loveable*; *movable* or *moveable*; *unmistakable* or *unmistakeable*.

If the word ends with the 'soft' *c* or *g* (as in *nice* or *huge*), the *e* is not omitted in front of *a* and *o*. Thus, *peace* and *service* give *peaceable* and *serviceable* respectively, while the *g* words *courage*, *manage*, and *outrage* produce the adjectives *courageous*, *manageable*, and *outrageous*.

The following words can be spelt with or without the *-e* after *g*: *acknowledgment* or *acknowledgement*; *judgment* or *judgement*.

In front of the suffixes that begin with a consonant, the final *-e* is not usually omitted: *arrange – arrangement*; *bore – boredom*; *complete – completely*; *precise – precisely*. Exceptions include: *argue – argument*; *due – duly*; *true – truly*.

'-our' and '-orous'

One of the best-known differences between British and American spelling affects words such as *humour*, which is spelt with two *u*'s in British and only one (*humor*) in American English. British users need to remember that the extra *u* is omitted when certain suffixes are added to them. The main suffix is *-ous*; others are *-ary*, *-ation*, *-ial*, and *-ific*. Thus *glamour – glamorous*; *humour – humorous*; *labour – laborious*; *colour – coloration*; *honour – honorary, honorific*; *armour – armorial*.

'-able' and '-ible'

It is often difficult to decide or remember which of these two forms of essentially the same suffix is the correct one to use when spelling a particular word. Of the two, *-able* is much the commoner. It stands to reason, therefore, that, if pressed, one should opt for it rather than for -*ible*. Moreover, new words are formed by adding -*able* rather than -*ible*: *microwave* – *microwav(e)able*; *photocopy* – *photocopiable*.

There are a few rules of thumb, however, which can act as pointers to those words in which -*ible* is the correct spelling.

Cases where the main part of the word to which the suffix is attached is not a complete and recognizable English word in itself tend to end in -*ible*. So we have *ed|ible*, *horr|ible*, and *terr|ible* and using the same system: *audible*, *credible*, *incredible*, and *visible* in contrast to, for example, *accept|able*, *agree|able*, *break|able*, and *work|able*. Unfortunately there are a good many exceptions to this rule, such as *affable*, *amenable*, *formidable*, *inevitable*, *memorable*, *probable*, and *vulnerable*.

Likewise, if the main part of the word ends in one of the following letters or combinations of letters then it is likely that -*ible* will be the correct form: a 'soft' *c* (*deducible*, *forcible*, *invincible*, *reducible*, *irascible*); a soft *g* (*eligible*, *incorrigible*, *legible*, *negligible*, *tangible*); the combinations *ns* and *ss* (*comprehensible*, *defensible*, *reprehensible*, *responsible*, *sensible*; *accessible*, *admissible*, *expressible*, *permissible*, *possible*). A good many words in which *ct*, *pt*, and *st* immediately precede the suffix also take -*ible* (*indestructible*; *contemptible*; *perceptible*; *digestible*, *inexhaustible*, and *irresistible*), but there are several -*able* words of this type as well, for example, *contactable*, *acceptable*, *adaptable*, and *detestable*.

Doubling of consonants

The principal spelling problem with consonants in English is to know when to double them. The basic rule is that when a word ends with a single consonant, that consonant doubles when adding a suffix which begins with a vowel. This applies to adjectives when adding *-er* and *-est* to form the comparative and superlative: *big – bigger – biggest*; *sad – sadder – saddest*. It applies to verbs forming their participles: *stop – stopping – stopped*; *tip – tipping – tipped*. It similarly applies when adding other suffixes to form different classes of words: *bid – biddable*; *plod – plodder*. It also applies when *-y* is added to form adjectives from nouns: *fun – funny*; *jam – jammy*; *wit – witty*.

All the above examples show words with only one syllable. When a word has two or more syllables, the rule still applies when the last syllable is stressed and the final consonant is preceded by a single vowel: *allot – allotting – allotted*; *commit – committing – committed – committal*; *compel – compelling – compelled*; *forget – forgetting – forgettable*; *occur – occurring – occurred*; *regret – regretting – regretted – regrettable*. Examples of words with more than two syllables: *disinter – disinterring – disinterred*; *intermit – intermittent*.

If the stress falls on an earlier syllable, the final consonant does not double. So *develop* (stress on the second syllable of three) has words deriving from it such as *developing, developed*, and *developer*; *focus – focused*; *benefit – benefited*; *target – targeted*. Occasionally, certain of these words may appear with a doubled consonant: *biassed, focussed, benefitted, targetted*, although these spellings are becoming less frequently used in contemporary English.

Exceptions include words that have a final *-l* which is doubled even though the syllable is unstressed: *travel – travelled – traveller*; *cancel – cancelled*; *counsel – counselled*. American spelling is more consistent than British in this respect, since all the above words have only one *l* (*traveler, counseled*, etc.) when spelt the American way. Other exceptions: *handicap – handicapped*; *worship – worshipped – worshipper* (American English usually *worshiped, worshiper*).

Difficult words

To end this section, here is a list of nearly 200 words, as spelt in British English, many not mentioned previously, that commonly cause problems. Other words that cause difficulty, e.g. *complimentary* and *complementary*, *disc* and *disk*, *licence* and *license*, *practice* and *practise*, *principal* and *principle*, are dealt with in chapter 2.

accessory

accommodate, accommodation

address

adolescent

advertisement

aggravate

all right

analyse, analysis

annihilate

anonymous

appalling

Arctic, Antarctic

asphyxiate

assassin, assassinate

assessment

attendant

bankruptcy

beautiful, beauty

besiege

bigot, bigoted

bourgeois

buoy, buoyant

caffeine

calendar

calibre

carburettor

catalogue

ceiling

census

chrysanthemum

commemorate

commiserate

committee

conceit

condemn

conscience, conscientious

conscious

consensus

copyright

corollary

correspondence, correspondent

deceive

descendant

desiccated

desperate

dialogue

diarrhoea

diphtheria

diphthong

discipline

ecstasy, ecstatic

eighth

embarrass

exaggerate

excite, exciting

exhilarate

Fahrenheit

fascinate

fatigue

favourite

February

fluorescent

forty

four, fourth

friend

fulfil

gardener

gauge

gorilla

gossip

government

grammar

guarantee

guard, guardian

guerrilla

haemorrhage

harass, harassment

height

honorary

hygiene

hypocrisy, hypocrite

idiosyncrasy

illegible

independent

inoculate

instalment

it's (it is)

its (of it)

leisure

liaise, liaison

liquefy

loose

lose

manoeuvre

Mediterranean

millennium

minuscule

miscellaneous

mortgage

moustache

necessarily, necessary

niece

occasion

ophthalmic,
   ophthalmologist

orthopaedic

oscillate

parallel

peccadillo

penicillin

perceive

perennial

personnel

playwright

pneumatic

possess

precede

privilege

proceed

psychiatry

psychology

pursue

questionnaire

queue, queued

receipt

recommend

reconnaissance

reconnoitre

relevant

rendezvous

repertoire

repetition

resistant

restaurant

resuscitate

rhyme

rhythm

right

sacrilegious

salutary

schizophrenia

seize

separate, separation

sergeant

sheikh

sheriff

siege

skilful

sober

sombre

straight

subterranean

supersede

surgeon

surveillance

susceptible

symmetrical, symmetry

synchronize

syringe

teetotaller

thief

threshold

tranquillizer

treacherous

vaccinate

vacillate

vacuum

variegated

Wednesday

weight

welcome

welfare

wholly

withhold

woollen

write

yacht

yoghurt/yogurt

4   Punctuation

Introduction

Punctuation breaks up the flow of words and thoughts into meaningful units. Without punctuation, a string of words would often remain just that – a string of words. Punctuation shapes sentences, distinguishes between different types of utterance, and highlights and emphasizes different words or groups of words. In proficiency in a language, knowledge and skill in the use of punctuation is as important as a sound grasp of grammar and a wide vocabulary.

It is easy enough to illustrate the confusion that can arise when punctuation marks are incorrectly used:

The supervisor said John was not doing his job properly.

This is a perfectly good and understandable sentence. Inserting two commas, however, can completely reverse its meaning:

The supervisor, said John, was not doing his job properly.

Adding quotation marks reinforces this interpretation of the sentence:

'The supervisor,' said John, 'was not doing his job properly.'

In dealing with punctuation, of course, we are concerned only with the written language. If sentences such as those used in the example above were spoken, it would be obvious which meaning was intended from the slight pauses that the speaker introduced, the way that their voice rose and fell, and the emphasis they put on different words. The human voice is a very flexible and expressive instrument. Body language and eye contact can also play their part. There are all sorts of ways in which meaning can be conveyed when speaking that are not available to someone who is using a pen or a keyboard and who cannot be heard or seen by the person that they are communicating with. Punctuation cannot be a substitute for all of these, but it can take the place of many of them. Good punctuation can almost put a shrug of the shoulders or a hesitant tone of voice down on paper without having to describe either explicitly. Imaginative and varied punctuation gives individual rhythm to a piece of prose.

Writers nowadays tend to punctuate their work much more lightly than they did in the past. Semicolons and colons were often used in places where nowadays many writers would put a comma, and commas were often used where most modern writers would put no punctuation at all. Dickens' sentences, for instance, sometimes seem to bristle with punctuation. This is the opening of *Nicholas Nickleby*:

> There once lived, in a sequestered part of the county of Devonshire, one Mr. Godfrey Nickleby: a worthy gentleman, who, taking it into his head rather late in life that he must get married, and not being young enough or rich enough to aspire to the hand of a lady of fortune, had wedded an old flame out of mere attachment, who in her turn had taken him for the same reason.

The bristly effect is even more pronounced in writers of earlier centuries. Here is the famous essayist Joseph Addison, one of the most admired stylists of his time, writing about Shakespeare in *The Spectator* in the early eighteenth century:

> Among great Genius's, those few draw the Admiration of
> mankind of all the World upon them, and stand up as the
> Prodigies of Mankind, who by the mere strength of natural
> Parts, and without any Assistance of Art or Learning, have
> produced Works that were the Delight of their own Times and
> the Wonder of Posterity.

Lighter punctuation goes with the plainer and rather more informal style adopted by most modern writers. It is perfectly possible to write quite long sentences which are structured so that they require no punctuation at all. The aim of this chapter is to give guidelines on correct and effective punctuation.

The comma

The comma is perhaps rivalled only by the apostrophe for the amount of confusion it can cause. In certain circumstances, including or excluding a comma is largely a matter of taste. There are many contexts, however, in which the correct use of a comma, as of any other punctuation mark, is essential if a sentence is to be properly understood.

Although the main function of punctuation is to separate – sentence from sentence, clause from clause, one meaningful unit of language from another – it can also be seen as a linking device. Commas illustrate this point well. They have several main functions – three that have mainly to do with separation and two that have more to do with linking. Commas separate the items in a list, separate small sections at the beginning and end of sentences, and bracket independent sections in the middle of sentences. But commas also link the clauses that make up a compound sentence and the beginning and end of clauses from which something has been missed out. These five functions will now be dealt with in more detail. Three other specific uses of commas will then complete this section.

Commas in lists

In lists, commas are generally a substitute for the word *and* and sometimes for the word *or*. They are used when a list contains three or more items which are single words, phrases, or sentences:

> *I bought apples, bananas, carrots, and lettuces.*
>
> *French is spoken in Canada, in North Africa, and in the Lebanon.*
>
> *The President speaks French, the Vice-President speaks German, and the Prime Minister speaks Greek.*

To repeat the point, these commas could, at least theoretically, be replaced by *and* (*I bought apples and bananas and carrots and lettuces*). If a comma in a list cannot be replaced by *and*, then it is in the wrong place.

It is becoming more common in British English (and is usual in American English) to place a comma before the *and* that precedes the final item in a simple list (*numbers one, two, three, and four*). A comma used in that position is known as a **serial comma**. This book uses such serial commas.

The more complex a list becomes, the more useful it is to add a serial comma: *The President speaks French, the Vice-President speaks German, and the Prime Minister speaks Greek.* There are also occasions when it is vital to use an extra comma because otherwise the divisions between the various items in the list might not be clear: *I've bought several recordings by Bob Dylan, Paul Simon, and*

Simon and Garfunkel. If there were no comma after *Paul Simon*, the reader might be misled into thinking there was a pop group called *Paul Simon and Simon and Garfunkel*.

Commas are also used to divide up lists of adjectives preceding a noun: *The suspect had long, dark, greasy hair*. It would, however, be equally correct in this case to omit the commas from the list entirely and to write: *The suspect had long dark greasy hair*. The use of commas, therefore, is common, but optional, in lists of adjectives that are all of equal value and all refer to the same noun.

Sometimes it is positively wrong to put in a comma. Take, for example, the sentences: *I bought two large, juicy, green apples* and *I bought two large, juicy green peppers*. In the first instance, *and* could be reasonably inserted in the list: *I bought two large and juicy and green apples*, or, more elegantly, *I bought two apples that were large and juicy and green*. All the adjectives refer equally to *apples*. In the second instance, what we assume the speaker bought was *two green peppers that were large and juicy* rather than *two peppers that were large and juicy and green*. In this instance, instead of three equal adjectives, we have two adjectives, *large* and *juicy*, preceding a compound noun *green pepper*.

Further, commas should not be placed between an adverb and an adjective. It is easy to make that mistake with adverbs such as *bright* or *hard* that have the same form as adjectives: compare *a bright, yellow moon* with *a bright yellow envelope*. Neither, generally speaking, should a comma be put in front of a noun used adjectivally in front of another noun: *a red, waxy substance* but a *red wax candle*.

Commas with clauses at beginnings and ends of sentences

When a subordinate clause begins a sentence, a comma is often used to separate it from the rest of the sentence:

> *When you next go to Paris, come and see me.*
>
> *Although he didn't like her, he was prepared to tolerate her.*
>
> *Since you're so clever, why don't you sort the whole thing out yourself?*

In these examples there is no great danger of the sense being misunderstood if the comma is omitted.

But where a subordinate clause ends with a verb, and the following clause begins with a noun, the danger of at least momentary confusion is greater. The insertion of a comma in such sentences is vital. Consider the following examples:

> *If they don't return, the money will be given to charity.*
>
> *After she had finished reading, the book was replaced on the shelf.*
>
> *As you see, the situation is desperate.*

In each case, the comma indicates that the writer intends the verb to be understood as an intransitive one (with no direct object). Remove the comma and it seems for a moment that the verb has a direct object after all:

> *If they don't return the money . . .*
>
> *After she had finished reading the book . . .*

As you see the situation . . .

A comma is also often used when an adverb, adverbial phrase, or adverbial clause comes at the beginning of a sentence. Here, too, it is often vital to insert a comma so that the sense can be properly understood. Consider the following examples:

Below, the ocean waves were crashing against the rocks.

Normally, intelligent people can see through such subterfuge.

After eating, the staff went home.

After a period of calm, college students have begun to demonstrate again.

If commas were left out of these sentences, the sense is different:

Below the ocean waves . . .

Normally intelligent people . . .

After eating the staff . . .

After a period of calm college students . . .

Even where there is no real danger of confusion or absurdity, it is usually better to insert a comma than not. Most phrases that are based on the infinitive form of a verb or a participle require one:

To do them justice, they were very apologetic.

Reading between the lines, I think they're getting very worried.

Having dealt with that problem successfully, she immediately turned her attention to the next.

Turning to the other end of the sentence, a comma is often used before a subordinate clause positioned after a main clause:

> *I'm very fond of him, although I'm well aware that he has his faults.*

> *Barbara couldn't come, because she had a prior engagement.*

A comma is not always necessary, however, in such sentences.

Commas are not used before clauses beginning with *that*:

> *It is possible that the delivery of the goods might be late.*

> *She told me that the rumours were untrue.*

> *There is a good chance that he will be out of hospital next week.*

The grammatical reason for this is that the *that* clauses in the above examples are functioning either as complements or, in the second example, as the object of the verb. It is, of course, proper to use commas to separate a series or 'list' of *that* clauses: *He said that he was sorry, that he hadn't meant to hurt anyone, that he'd paid for any damage, and that he hoped we would forgive him.*

Finally, commas are always used after a group of words that makes a statement when a tag question such as *didn't he* or *aren't they* is tacked onto it:

> *It's nice and warm today, isn't it?*

> *You are coming out tonight, aren't you?*

Bracketing commas

One of the most important functions of commas is their use in pairs to separate a piece of information that is obviously additional to the main meaning of a sentence. In fact, such pieces of information are not merely additional; they are, strictly speaking, superfluous to the sentence as a whole. They can be removed from it and the sentence will still make sense.

For example, take the sentence *David Mander, the club's new chairperson, made a speech*. Here the phrase *the club's new chairperson* describes David Mander, but is essentially incidental to the main statement, which is that *David Mander made a speech*. The sentence could be switched around – in this case making the name of the new chairperson the incidental factor – and the punctuation would remain the same: *The club's new chairperson, David Mander, made a speech*. Here are some examples where the insert is much longer, but it is nonetheless incidental to the sentence as a whole and so is enclosed within commas:

> *It's not the most beautiful car in the world, as anyone can see, but it is very economical.*

> *The dictionary, first published in 1918 and re-edited at roughly ten-year intervals ever since, has never been out of print.*

> *Gone are the days when, because everything Victorian was out of fashion, such buildings were considered to be a joke.*

There are all sorts of little phrases that commonly occur within sentences – *above all; as I said; in fact; of course; what is more*, etc. – that should, in most instances, appear only within commas:

He felt, of course, rather foolish.

I, in fact, had said much the same thing at a previous meeting.

The terms they were offering were, to be honest, less favourable than we had expected.

In a similar way there are a number of single words, often serving as backward links to what has been said in a previous sentence, to which the same thing applies. *However* is perhaps the most common:

The railway system, however, remains in a state of disrepair.

The board, consequently, has had to revise its previous decision.

We have, nevertheless, to consider the other possibilities.

A major source of trouble with commas lies in their use in what are known as **non-restrictive clauses** – that is, those that describe rather than identify (or define) a person or thing (see also pp. 24–6). Because such clauses *describe* rather than *identify*, they could be omitted, and so they go into commas. The problem is to decide what identifies and what merely describes.

Consider the example: *My sister who lives in Australia is a sales executive*. There are two ways of understanding and, consequently, of punctuating this sentence. The first assumes that the sentence refers specifically to *my sister who lives in Australia*. The implication is that the speaker has more than one sister. One lives in Australia, the others live elsewhere, consequently the phrase *who lives in Australia* identifies and defines which sister is being talked about. The phrase is, therefore, crucial to the sentence and *cannot* be put between commas. The second way of understanding the sentence, however, is that it refers simply to *my sister* – possibly the speaker's only sister – who is a sales executive. In that case, the fact that she lives in Australia is a piece of incidental information and the phrase that expresses this should be enclosed in commas: *My sister, who lives in Australia, is a sales executive.*

When referring to things, non-restrictive (describing) clauses always begin with *which* and restrictive (identifying or defining) clauses may begin with either *that* or *which*. Note too that *that* clauses do not have commas; *which* clauses frequently do.

Here are some further examples:

> Mrs Beeton's Book of Household Management, *which was first published in 1861, has become an international bestseller.*

The clause *which was first published in 1861* gives incidental information and so is a non-restrictive *which* clause, with commas.

> *The cookery book that I had been given as a birthday present somehow got lost in the move.*

This is a restrictive *that* clause – it identifies or defines which cookery book – and so there are no commas.

A further type of descriptive relative clause that is used with a comma is one in which the *which* clause relates to the main clause as a whole.

> *He failed the exam, which was not surprising.*
>
> *They helped us move house, for which we were most grateful.*

Linking commas

Commas are often used to link together the two parts of a compound sentence, a compound sentence being one that has two main clauses joined by *and*, *or*, *but*, *yet*, or *while* (see pp. 17–18). However, it is as important to know when not to use a comma as when to use one.

When the two clauses have the same subject or initial phrase, whether or not it is repeated, a comma is not usually used:

> *They speak Italian fluently and (they) can get by in Spanish as well.*

> *On the stroke of midnight Cinderella's fine clothes turned back into rags and (also on the stroke of midnight) her silver coach vanished into thin air.*

When the subjects of the two clauses joined by *and* or *or* are not the same, however, a comma is generally used:

> *They speak fluently, and their Italian friends are equally fluent in English.*

> *Is that your final decision, or do you need more time to think things over?*

A comma is particularly used when the two clauses form a contrast:

> *Jan wants to continue the relationship, but Tom wants to walk out and end it.*

> *It seems like a good idea, yet I'm not at all convinced it will work.*

The use of the comma has the effect of highlighting the contrast and also making a slight pause between the clauses. Nevertheless, if the clauses are fairly short, the comma is optional: *The car overturned but the driver wasn't hurt.*

If there are two clauses in the sentence, and they are not joined by *and*, etc., then a comma is not usually the correct way to link them. If their meaning is quite closely connected, a semicolon (see also pp. 181–3) should be used instead of a comma: *German-born Schmidt became a British citizen; he later married an English-woman.*

Where the meaning is less closely connected, the better alternative is to have two sentences: *The red car was cheaper. The blue car, on the other hand, looked much smarter.*

Commas filling gaps

Sometimes a group of words (usually a verb phrase) that is used in one clause needs to be repeated in a subsequent clause in order to complete its sense. But if repeating the phrase would make the sentence very cumbersome, it can be omitted, and a comma inserted in its place. Take, for example: *They had already made a decision to go; we had already made a decision to stay.* The phrase *had already made a decision* can be replaced in the second clause by a comma, producing a much crisper result: *They had already made a decision to go; we, to stay.* The comma also has the same function in the following sentences:

> *Chelsea had the greater share of possession in the first half; Villa, in the second.*
>
> *The new building was generally considered to be an eyesore,*

> *the exhibition, a failure, and the whole enterprise, a waste of*
> *public money.*
>
> *To err is human, to forgive, divine.*

Commas and speech

A comma is used between the words of direct speech – the words that are put in quotation marks – and the verb *say* or any other reporting expression:

> *'Come and look at the room,' he said, 'it has a sea view.'*
>
> *'I'm back,' she called out.*
>
> *He ventured the question, 'Do you really love me?'*

For more on this, see pp. 186–9.

Remember, however, that a comma is not used before *that*, etc. in indirect speech:

> *She called out that she was back.*
>
> *The committee agreed that they would fund half the cost of*
> *the extension.*

Commas with numbers

Commas are used to divide large numbers into groups of three digits, to separate thousands, millions, etc.:

> *65,678*
>
> *10,137,673*

Note that commas are sometimes not used with four-digit

numbers and they are never used in dates: *4,517* or *4517*; *in the year 2010.*

Spaces are sometimes used in place of commas, particularly with metric units: *A kilometre consists of 1 000 metres.*

Commas with names

Commas must be used when a person is being addressed by name or when a group of people are being addressed:

> *Please, Fred, try again.*
>
> *Sergeant Miller, take those men away.*
>
> *Ladies and gentlemen, boys and girls, welcome to the show.*
>
> *I've told you before, Hoskins, this has got to stop.*

The reason for this is simple and goes back to what has been said before. Without commas, the name appears as part of the sentence. Compare *I'm fed up with ringing Jane* and *I'm fed up with ringing, Jane.*

The full stop

There are two functions of the full stop. Its main one is to mark the end of a sentence that does not have a question mark or an exclamation mark at the end. This function does not require specific illustration. Most of the sentences in this book end with full stops. It is worth noting, however, that a sentence should never have more than one full stop. This rule mainly comes into play in relation to quotations: see pp. 186–9.

A full stop is also used with certain types of abbreviation, though generally it must be said that full stops are used less with abbreviations these days than in the past. The abbreviation for the 'British Broadcasting Corporation' is now more commonly found as *BBC* than *B.B.C.* Full stops tend to be used more with abbreviations that consist of small letters, particularly when the abbreviated form without the full stops could be confused with an ordinary word: *a.m.* (ante meridiem, before noon), *f.o.b.* (free on board, relating to a shipment of goods); *e.g.* (exempli gratia, for example).

Abbreviations which contain the first and last letters of a word (*Mr*; *St* (Saint or Street)) are generally written without a full stop.

The question mark

The question mark has one main function: to appear at the end of a direct question and indicate that it is a question:

> *Which way is it to the station?*
>
> *So Margot has invited you too, has she?*
>
> *He did what?*

When a sentence ends in a question mark, it does not require a full stop.

There are several different ways in which questions can be phrased in standard English. These are dealt with on pp. 13–15 and pp. 46–7. Any question that is addressed directly to another person needs a question mark. So does any rhetorical question, that is, one to which an answer is not really expected:

> *How do you do?*
>
> *Where has the time gone?*

How can people live like that?

So too does a question that is reported in direct speech: *'Have you seen my book anywhere?' he asked.* Notice that in this instance the question mark is placed inside the inverted commas.

The only type of question that does not require a question mark is a question that is given in reported (or indirect) speech. (See also pp. 22–4.) It would be incorrect to end any of the following examples with a question mark:

> *She asked me why I had come.*
>
> *People are very curious to know how you managed to do it.*
>
> *We questioned him again as to what had motivated his decision.*

The presence of question words (*why, how, what*) in these sentences does not alter the fact that they are essentially statements giving information rather than questions requesting it.

The question mark has one minor function, which is to indicate that something, often a date or figure, is doubtful or an estimate. When used in this way the question mark usually appears next to (usually in front of) whatever it refers to. Often the question mark is put inside brackets. For example, the year in which the poet Geoffrey Chaucer died is known precisely, but the year of his birth is not, so his dates are often shown in the following form: *Geoffrey Chaucer (?1342–1400)*. Likewise the question mark in the following example shows that the speaker is not precisely sure what number is involved: *According to the rules, 33 per cent of committee members constitute a quorum, that is (?)9 people* (or *?9 people*).

The exclamation mark

The exclamation mark is another punctuation mark with one main function – to indicate that the words that precede it constitute an exclamation:

> *How splendid!*
>
> *Give me a chance!*
>
> *Stand still!*
>
> *What a disaster!*

As with the question mark, a sentence ending in an exclamation mark does not need a full stop. Likewise, an exclamation reported in direct speech ends with an exclamation mark inside the inverted commas: *'What an extraordinary coincidence!' he exclaimed.*

The nature and form of exclamations is discussed on p. 16. Exclamations are usually fairly short expressions of heightened emotion which are often given in a somewhat louder voice than ordinary speech. Since formal writing generally adopts a moderate tone, the use of exclamation marks in formal writing is comparatively rare. In fact, most writers on punctuation discourage the use of too many exclamation marks, suggesting that, if used too frequently, they give a piece of writing an overheated and hysterical or slightly bullying tone. They also frown on the use of more than one exclamation mark at a time (*Goal!!!*). This is good advice for formal writing, though in personal or comic writing this rule can be relaxed.

Exclamation marks are also occasionally used to draw attention to an interruption – often one enclosed in brackets or between dashes – in the general flow of a sentence, especially if the interruption is a slightly ironical one:

On those (thankfully rare!) occasions when we tried to have a
serious conversation . . .

Our visitors arrived at noon – Jean wasn't up yet! – having
been invited for six o'clock in the evening.

The semicolon

The semicolon, like the colon, is probably underused as a punctuation mark because its correct use is felt to be complicated and
difficult. This is not, in fact, the case: the basic rule for using the
semicolon is quite simple. It links together clauses which could
stand alone as sentences, but which have a close relationship with
one another and are more effectively shown as components of a
single sentence. Semicolons are not used in conjunction with
linking words such as *and* or *but*; they are, however, frequently
used in situations where an alternative method of constructing
the sentence would be to use a joining word of that kind.

The basic point to remember is that semicolons join clauses that
could function as complete sentences. If a clause cannot function
as a complete sentence, it ought, generally speaking, not to begin
or end with a semicolon. Let us look at a few examples:

John was wearing his best suit; Mary was in a T-shirt and a
pair of torn jeans.

The troops are preparing to attack the city; all foreign
journalists have been ordered to leave the area.

The prime minister sat down; the leader of the opposition
stood up; a sudden hush fell over the chamber.

In all the above examples, clearly, the elements that make up the sentences could stand alone as sentences:

> *John was wearing his best suit.*

> *Mary was in a T-shirt and a pair of torn jeans.*

> *All foreign journalists have been ordered to leave the area.*

> *The leader of the opposition stood up.*

What may not be quite so clear is why it is desirable to use a semicolon in such sentences instead of full stops or a conjunction such as *and*. The answer lies in the second part of the rule given in the first paragraph of this section. A semicolon links clauses which could stand alone, but which have a close relationship with one another and are more effectively shown as components of a single sentence. To look at it from the opposite viewpoint, the use of a semicolon rather than a full stop implies a relationship between the two clauses which the semicolon joins.

Take the first of the examples shown above. If it reads as follows:

> *John was wearing his best suit.*

> *Mary was in a T-shirt and a pair of torn jeans.*

then these two sentences might simply be part of a string of similar sentences describing the clothes worn by all the people present on a particular occasion. Using a semicolon implies that the facts that John was dressing up and that Mary was dressing down are somehow related – perhaps that they are a couple with different attitudes to dress. An alternative way of constructing this same sentence would be to use *and*: *John was wearing his best suit, and Mary was in a T-shirt and a pair of torn jeans*. This is a perfectly good sentence. The only difference between it and the sentence with the semicolon is that it is slightly less crisp and the contrast is slightly less pointed. The semicolon is particularly well adapted to point up the contrast between two otherwise related statements: *It was the shortest day of the year; it felt like the longest day of my life.*

The situation is slightly different with regard to the third example:

> *The prime minister sat down; the leader of the opposition stood up; a sudden hush fell over the chamber.*

This sentence would obviously be rather clumsy if two *ands* were inserted into it. The choice is really between dividing it with semicolons or with full stops. The difference is a slight one, but worth noting. To use full stops would tend to interrupt the narrative flow more, describing, as it were, three separate actions. To use semicolons and keep the description of the three actions within one sentence suggests that they were all part of the same process – one incident with three parts, rather than three separate incidents.

The semicolon is also used as a stronger dividing mark in lists, particularly lists whose component elements use commas for internal punctuation. In this particular case, it is not necessary for the elements divided by semicolons to be possible complete sentences: *There are three courses I can particularly recommend: 'Computing for Beginners', run by Ms Jenkins, which is aimed at absolute novices; 'How Your Computer Works', a course that deals, basically, with the hardware side of things and is run by Mr Watt; 'Intermediate-Level Computing', also by Ms Jenkins, which requires a certain amount of previous knowledge, but should not be beyond your capabilities.*

The colon

The use of the colon in modern English is, like that of the semi-colon, rather simpler than it is often imagined to be. The main use of the colon is to separate a general statement from one or more statements or items that give more specific information and illustrate or explain it:

> *There are three reasons why I'm not coming with you: I haven't the time, I haven't the money, and I don't like skiing.*

The general statement (*There are three reasons . . .*) is followed by a simple explanation of what those reasons are.

> *Economists have a lot in common with weather-forecasters: they are often wrong* (The Guardian).

There is no need for the item or items that follow the colon to be complete sentences:

> *They knew precisely what they were facing: almost certain death.*

> *Two members of the committee have already been named: Mrs Atkinson and Mr Peters.*

> *The effect of the explosion were all too visible: houses burning, glass littering the street, people wandering around in a state of shock.*

The colon is also sometimes used to introduce a passage of direct speech: *Mr Harris said, and I quote: 'The whole thing has been a complete waste of time and money.'* This, however, is a convention mainly used in journalism. Most authorities recommend using a comma at the beginning of a passage of direct speech (see pp. 186–9).

Quotation marks

Quotation marks (also known as inverted commas) are primarily used to indicate that the words written between the *opening* (' or ") and the *closing* (' or ") marks are the words that the person in question has actually spoken:

> *He said, 'I'm ready now.'*
>
> *'What are you doing here?' she asked.*
>
> *'Time,' Groucho Marx is supposed to have said, 'wounds all heels.'*

Quotations from a piece of writing also need to be placed inside inverted commas:

> *We felt we were dealing with what St Paul referred to as 'spiritual wickedness in high places'.*
>
> *In your report you mention 'an undercurrent of hostility towards management among the workforce'. What precisely did you mean by that?*

Only the words that were actually spoken or written by the person in question belong inside quotation marks. All the other words should be left outside, even if they come in the middle of the remark being actually quoted and so necessitate the use of two sets of quotation marks:

> *'Time,'* Groucho Marx is supposed to have said, *'wounds all heels.'*

> *'My darling,'* he wrote in a letter hurriedly scribbled just before boarding the plane, *'I wish you knew how much I love you.'*

Double or single quotation marks

There is no difference in meaning or use between single quotation marks ('. . .') and double ones (". . ."). The most important thing is to choose a system and adhere to it consistently. Most British book publishers prefer the use of single *quotes* (quotation marks), reserving the use of double quotes for quotations within quotations: *'What Shakespeare actually wrote,'* Harry interrupted, *'was "We are such stuff as dreams are made on", not "made of", as you seem to think.'* If the quotation within a quotation happens to fall at the end of a sentence then two sets of quotation marks will be needed: *She noted, 'I wish he wouldn't call me "duck".'* In the US double quotes are used as the primary level and single quotes are used for the secondary level of quotations within quotations.

Punctuation with quotation marks

While the rules governing what should go into quotation marks are fairly simple, the rules governing how other punctuation should be used in conjunction with them are more complicated.

A comma is used with the verb of reporting to separate the unspoken words and the spoken words:

> *He said, 'I'm ready now.'*

'I've no idea what you're talking about,' she replied.

She leapt up out of her chair and shouted, 'I can smell something burning.'

When the reporting verb is placed in the middle of a quotation, commas perform their usual bracketing function:

'Time,' Groucho Marx is supposed to have said, 'wounds all heels.'

'That,' she replied, 'is a matter of opinion.'

It will be noted that in each of these examples the first comma has been placed inside the quotation marks.

If the words being quoted make a full sentence, then the passage within quotation marks should begin with a capital letter and end with a full stop: *He said, 'You deliberately lied to me.'* The same applies if the words quoted form a question or an exclamation:

She merely smiled and enquired, 'Where have you been hiding all this while?'

The man behind me roared out, 'Stop that infernal noise!'

The full stop, question mark, and exclamation mark all come before the closing quotation mark. It is incorrect to place an additional full stop outside the closing quotation mark.

When the quoted words do not form a full sentence, then there should be no capital letter and the full stop should appear outside the inverted commas because it belongs to the sentence in which the quotation appears, not to the quotation itself:

They both wrote saying that they wanted to 'try and sort things out between them'.

> *The expression 'to out-herod Herod' means 'to exceed someone in a particular quality', especially wickedness or cruelty.*

American usage differs from British usage at this point. In American usage, full stops and commas come inside the quotation marks:

> *They both wrote saying that they wanted to "try and sort things out between them."*

> *The expression "to out-herod Herod" means "to exceed someone in a particular quality," especially wickedness or cruelty.*

In both British and American English, semicolons and colons come outside the quotation marks:

> *A critical phase is reached as the aircraft goes 'transonic'; that is, as it accelerates through the speed band from just below to just above the speed of sound.* (New Scientist)

> *A common method of cheating is to rely on what magicians call a "stooge": someone who is watching behind a screen and sending secret signals to the psychic by any one of scores of little-known techniques.* (Scientific American)

The position of the question mark and exclamation mark depends on whether they belong to the quoted material or not:

> *Did he really say, 'I wish I hadn't married you'?*

> *He asked, 'Is it time for me to go yet?'*

> *She had the cheek to say to me, 'I never want to see you*
> *again'!*

> *The man behind me roared out, 'Stop that infernal noise!'*

Quotation marks and paragraphs

In a passage of dialogue, each act of speech normally starts a new paragraph:

> *'You know,' he said, in an important voice, 'I've thought all along*
> *that that pig of ours was an extra good one. He's a solid pig. That*
> *pig is as solid as they come. You notice how solid he is around the*
> *shoulders, Lurvy?'*
> *'Sure, sure I do,' said Lurvy. 'I've always noticed that pig. He's*
> *quite a pig.'*
> *'He's long, and he's smooth,' said Zuckerman.*
> *'That's right,' agreed Lurvy. 'He's as smooth as they come. He's*
> *some pig.'*
> (from E. B. White, *Charlotte's Web*)

If a quoted passage consists of more than one paragraph, opening quotation marks are placed at the beginning of each paragraph, but the closing quotation marks are placed only at the end of the complete quotation, i.e. at the end of the final paragraph:

> *'Woe to you Pharisees, because you give God a tenth of your mint,*
> *rue and all other kinds of garden herbs, but you neglect justice and*
> *the love of God. You should have practised the latter without leaving*
> *the former undone.*
> *'Woe to you Pharisees, because you love the most important seats*
> *in the synagogues and greetings in the market-places.*

> *'Woe to you, because you are like unmarked graves, which men walk over without knowing it.'*
> (The Bible, Luke 11:42–4, New International Version, London, Hodder & Stoughton Ltd)

Quotation marks in titles

Quotation marks are also used for certain titles, for example, of essays, songs and of alternative names of musical works:

> *The Beatles' song* 'She Loves You'
>
> *Mozart's Symphony no. 38 in D, K504* ('Prague')
>
> *David Smith,* 'Recent Developments in German', *Journal of Modern Languages, 51 (1995), pp. 143–6*

Quotation marks used to create a distance

Quotation marks are also sometimes placed around words or phrases that were not actually spoken or written by a specific other person, but which represent the point of view of another person or other people rather than the writer's own. The effect of using them is to create a distance from the word or phrase, often, in effect, saying, 'He, she, or they may call it that, but I wouldn't.' For example: *Apparently his 'hobbies' include bungee-jumping and fire-walking.* The implication is that those two activities are most peculiar things to call hobbies. The use of quotation marks in this way often suggests disapproval of, or an ironic or sarcastic attitude towards, the thing or phrase in question: *I've never been anyone's 'significant other', to the best of my knowledge, and I don't intend to start now.*

Highlighting particular words

Quotation marks are also used to highlight a particular phrase and, as it were, extract it from its immediate context:

> *'People' is a plural noun.*
>
> *It is possible to use either a singular or a plural verb with the word 'statistics'.*
>
> *Are there two m's in 'accommodation'?*

The dash

The function of the dash is similar to that of the bracketing comma, in that it is frequently used in pairs to separate an inserted item or interruption from the rest of the sentence. A dash is, however, a far stronger punctuation mark than a comma, and a more eye-catching one. It is best used for fairly dramatic and large-scale interruptions in the middle of sentences: *The thieves – there were four of them, all masked and brandishing heavy iron bars – forced the terrified sales assistants to lie down on the floor.* The size of the insert (*there were four of them, all masked and brandishing heavy iron bars*) and the fact that it constitutes a complete sentence on its own make it impossible to accommodate within commas. Consequently, dashes are needed. Here is a similar example: *Mr Brown – Why is there someone like Mr Brown in every single class I ever teach? – was still having trouble finding the shift key.* There is no other way, apart from using round brackets, of accommodating a complete question within another sentence.

The dash is not, however, limited to use with such lengthy inserts:

> *There was no reason – at least, none that I could see – why we had to go through the whole rigmarole again.*

> *The point is – and this is the crux of the matter – that if we don't get additional funding, we shall have to close.*

A dash can also be used singly to separate the end of a sentence: again, usually in order to establish a fairly marked contrast, between it and what has gone before. It marks where there is a change of tone (or where there would be a change in the speaker's tone of voice if the sentence were spoken):

> *It would be a complete and utter disaster if they did that to us – not that I think for a moment that they will.*

> *It was a murder with an obvious motive and an obvious suspect – or so we thought.*

In all these instances, the dash is used with a space at either end of it. It can also be used, without spaces, to indicate a range of numbers or values, for example, when indicating a person's life-span (*Charles Dickens, 1812–70*) or the duration of a period (*the Jurassic period 208–146 million years ago*). Note that when the dash is used in this way, there is no need to use a construction with *from* and *to* or *between* and *and*. Write either *The compound contains 10–14 per cent potassium* or *The compound contains from 10 to 14 per cent potassium*, not *from 10–14 per cent*.

The hyphen: word-making

A hyphen makes words by joining together two existing words either permanently or, as it were, temporarily.

As is mentioned elsewhere in this book (pp. 115–16), the number of words with a permanent hyphen in English is tending gradually to diminish. It was not so long ago that even a word such as *today* was often spelt *to-day*. That spelling is now considered old-fashioned, but until very recently it was usual for prefixes that ended in a vowel to be attached with words that began with a vowel by means of a hyphen. This is no longer the situation: modern dictionaries give *antiaircraft* not *anti-aircraft*, *cooperate* before *co-operate*, *rearm* not *re-arm*, *socioeconomic* not *socio-economic*. The process is not complete, however. Apart from *cooperate* and *coordinate*, the tendency is still to hyphenate compound words where the prefix ends with the same vowel that the main word begins with (*anti-inflationary*; *pre-exist*; *re-establish*). Not that it is wrong to use a hyphen in words such as *anti-aircraft*, it is simply that the modern trend is against it and the tendency is either to make one solid compound word or to use two words. If in doubt, consult a modern dictionary.

The hyphen, however, is still widely used for 'temporary' word construction. By 'temporary' construction is meant for such words as *word-making* that has been used in the title of this section. It is a convenient and perfectly understandable term, made by joining two existing words together, but it would not appear in any dictionary. The particular word-making process involves taking material that might usually appear after the noun in question and placing it in front of it:

> *hyphens that make words – word-making hyphens*
>
> *a child who is two years old – a two-year-old child*
>
> *a region that produces grain – a grain-producing region*
>
> *a company that is not in business for profit – a not-for-profit company*

When they are used before a noun, such constructions should have hyphens. Probably the best-known and best-established words of this type in English are the *well* compounds. When they appear after a verb they have no hyphen; when they appear before a noun, they have one:

> *She is well known as a singer – She is a well-known singer.*
>
> *The fact is well established – a well-established fact.*

The insertion of hyphens when such combined words are used in front of nouns is a very helpful guide to the reader, who in this way knows what belongs together.

On the use of the hyphen with words beginning *non-*, see pp. 125–6 and with words beginning *re-* (e.g. *re-cover* ('cover again') and *recover* ('recuperate'), see p. 135.

Word-breaking hyphens

The word-breaking function of hyphens is usually more of an issue for a typesetter than for the ordinary writer. If a word will not fit onto a line, it is customary to break it with a hyphen, leaving part of the word and the hyphen on the first line and putting the remainder of the word on the next. This only applies to words of more than one syllable, and there are rather complicated rules determining at which points words may or may not be broken. Some ordinary dictionaries show the correct syllable breaks in words; all specialized spelling dictionaries do.

Hanging hyphens

There are two other minor uses of the hyphen. If, for any reason,
a writer only wishes to show part of a word, or a word component
such as a prefix or a suffix that is not complete in itself, then a
hyphen is attached to the beginning or the end of it:

> *The same applies to the prefix 'pre-'.*

> *Another common noun suffix is '-ment'.*

A hyphen can also be used when two words that share a
common second element are used close together, to shorten the
first and avoid the necessity of writing them both out twice. For
example, instead of writing *both the pro-hunting and anti-hunting
lobbies*, the following shortened version is acceptable: *both the pro-
and anti-hunting lobbies*. Likewise, instead of writing *She tried to
explain the distinction between metapsychology and parapsychology*,
the following shortened version is acceptable: *. . . the distinction
between meta- and parapsychology*.

Brackets: round

The function of round brackets (also known as *parentheses*) is much
the same as that of dashes and bracketing commas. They always
appear in pairs and put what is contained within them slightly
apart from the rest of the sentence. They are particularly useful
for marking asides from the writer to the reader:

> *It is said (though not by historians) that the tree was planted
> by King Charles I.*

> *If in doubt, consult a (modern) dictionary.*

They are also frequently used to enclose a small piece of explanatory or interpretative material:

> *Charles Dickens (1812–70)*

> *He showed me the recipe for* Sachertorte *(a type of Austrian chocolate cake).*

> *The World Health Organization (WHO) has its headquarters in Geneva.*

Square brackets

The most frequent function of square brackets is to enclose a brief comment inside a quotation, to clarify or specify something that is left vague or unspecified in the piece quoted:

> *The two authors she most admired [Charles Dickens and Sir Walter Scott] dealt with subjects very different to the ones she chose.*

Square brackets are also used to indicate that a mistake in the passage was made by the original author, not by the writer quoting the original text. The formula *[sic]* is used for this purpose:

> *He wrote, 'We are planning a big celebration for the millenium [sic].'*

> *'There is [sic] still a great many things to discuss.'*

The apostrophe: plurals

The apostrophe is never used to form the plurals of ordinary nouns. It seems to be becoming more and more common to see signs advertising, for example, *lettuce*'s or *sausage*'s or, perhaps slightly more forgivably, *CD's*. Apostrophe plurals have been occasionally spotted in subtitles for the television news. They are all incorrect. Ordinary nouns, even personal names, even names or nouns ending in *s*, do not need an apostrophe to form their plurals:

> *There are three other Janes in Jane's class.*

> *The team contained three Joneses and two Evanses.*

Abbreviations, when they have a plural, do not need an apostrophe either: *CDs or C.D.s*. Apostrophes are generally not now used, at least in British English, when referring to a particular decade of a century: *the 1990s; the 1820s*.

The only occasion on which an apostrophe should be used to make a plural is when one needs to refer in the plural to individual letters of the alphabet:

> *How many i's are there in 'Mississippi'?*

> *Are there two m's in 'accommodation'?*

There is obvious scope for confusion if the plurals of *a*, *i*, and *u* were to be written as *as*, *is*, and *us* respectively.

The apostrophe and the possessive

An apostrophe *s* (*'s*) is used to form the possessive of ordinary nouns in English: to show, in other words, that a particular thing or quality belongs to or is connected with someone or something. In the sentence *There are three other Janes in Jane's class*, *Janes* is the plural form of *Jane*, while *Jane's* is the possessive form.

The apostrophe *s* can be added to the end of almost all singular nouns (including those that end in *s*, add *-es* to form the plural, or consist of more than one word); *Jess'* (or *Jess's*) *notebook*; *the bus's numberplate*; *the church's one foundation*; *his mistress's voice*; *the vice captain's role*; *the Bath Investment and Building Society's head office*. Abbreviations too can take an apostrophe *s*: *an MP's salary*; *the TV's wiring system*.

When a noun forms its plural in the normal way by adding an *s* or *es*, the possessive is formed by adding an apostrophe only: *my parents' house*; *the parties' election manifestos*; *the Petersons' party*. The same goes for the plurals of abbreviations: *MPs' salaries*. If a noun has an irregular plural that ends in a letter other than *s*, then an apostrophe *s* is added as for the singular: *women's attitude to work*; *children's toys*; *the bureaux's permanent staffs*; *the media's coverage of the event*.

There are two exceptions to these general rules. The more important one relates to personal possessive pronouns. *Hers, ours, yours,* and *theirs* have no apostrophe. They may sound as if they might have (*hers* = *her* + apostrophe *s*), but they do not. If in doubt, remember that *his* and *mine* are the other two members of this particular class of words and there is no way in which either of them can accommodate an apostrophe. Remember also that a word with an apostrophe usually comes before the noun, whereas *hers, ours,* etc., come after it:

> *The handwriting is definitely hers.*

> *Those seats are ours.*

This last point is not invalidated by the existence of a rather unusual construction with *of* involving the possessive form, which is the second exception to the general rule: *a friend of mine*; *a photograph of Cecil Beaton's* (that is, taken by or belonging to Cecil

Beaton, in contrast to *a photograph of Cecil Beaton* – that is, depicting him).

'Its' and 'whose'

For many people, the most difficult possessive forms are *its* and *whose*. Because *its* is used before a noun, the temptation to give it an apostrophe is sometimes almost overwhelming. It does not have one:

> *The dog has lost its bone.*
>
> *Half its bits are missing.*
>
> *What have you done with its cover?*

There is a word *it's*, but it is a contraction of *it is*: see pp. 200–201. Similarly, there is a word *who's* meaning *who is* or *who has*, but the possessive form is *whose*:

> *Whose book is this?*
>
> *Whose are those gloves on the table?*
>
> *The people whose names are on the list . . .*

Names ending in '-s'

Usage varies with names ending in *s*. The style with only the apostrophe is possibly slightly more common than that with the apostrophe *'s*: *Robert Burns' poetry* or *Robert Burns's poetry*; *Henry James' novels* or *Henry James's novels*; *Keats' poems* or *Keats's poems*; *Diana Ross' recordings* or *Diana Ross's recordings*.

Apostrophes with nouns as modifiers

Finally, with the increasing use of nouns as modifiers before other nouns in modern English, it is difficult sometimes to decide whether there should be an apostrophe in a combination such as, for example, *trousers pocket*. Since you can say *the pocket of my trousers* it might be reasonable to suppose that *trousers' pocket* was correct. You could equally well say *the pocket of my jacket*, but nobody would say *it's in my jacket's pocket*. On the basis of comparison and analogy, therefore, it is reasonable to conclude that if *jacket pocket*, *coat pocket*, and *shirt pocket* are correct, then *trousers pocket* is correct as well. On the other hand, the combination *girls' changing room* is preferable to *girls changing room* on the basis that you would not speak of a *women* or *men changing room* but of a *women's* or *men's changing room*.

The apostrophe and contractions

The other main use of the apostrophe, besides indicating the possessive form of nouns, is to show that a letter has been missed out of a word. There are two main types of contraction. First, words in which the word *not* is next to a verb and part of *not* has been left out: *can't* = can not; *isn't* = is not; *don't* = do not, etc. Secondly, words in which a personal pronoun has been run together with a simple verb and part of the verb has been omitted: *I'm* = I am; *you've* = you have; *they'll* = they will, etc. All these forms are characteristic of speech and less formal writing. The apostrophe is a vital component of all these words: they are incorrectly spelt without it. In several cases there are other words with the identical spelling apart from the apostrophe: *were* and *we're*; *cant* and *can't*; *shell* and *she'll*; *hell* and *he'll*, etc. Although the spelling is different, there is perhaps an even greater risk of confusion between *you're* and *your*, and between *they're* and *their*, because these words are pronounced in the same way.

There are a number of other words which need an apostrophe of this kind – the commonest being *o'clock* (reduced from 'of the clock'). On the other hand, well-established cut-down forms of longer words do not need apostrophes: *bra*; *cello*; *flu*; *hippo*; *phone*. Other examples of words that need an apostrophe include *cat-o'-nine-tails*, *ne'er-do-well*, and *will-o'-the-wisp*. A number of archaic poetic forms require an apostrophe (*'tis* (it is); *'twere* (it were); *e'en* (even); *e'er* (ever); *ne'er* (never)). So, at the other end of the scale, do representations of very casual speech: *'Fraid I can't help you there*; *S'pose so*.

Glossary of grammatical terms

abbreviation A shortened form of a word, phrase, or title, used for convenience and to save space, e.g. *BBC* for 'British Broadcasting Corporation', *NATO* for 'North Atlantic Treaty Organization', *Dr* for 'doctor'.

abstract noun A noun that refers to something that cannot be seen and touched, e.g. *happiness* and *unity*. Compare **concrete noun**.

acronym A type of abbreviation that is made up of the initial letters of words and is pronounced as one word, e.g. *UNESCO* for 'United Nations Educational, Scientific, and Cultural Organization', and *laser* for 'light amplification by stimulated emission of radiation'.

active Used to describe a verb in which the subject of the sentence carries out the action described by the verb, e.g. *hit* in *He hit me*. Compare **passive**.

adjective A word that describes a person or thing more precisely by indicating a quality that he, she, or it possesses, e.g. *big*, *deep*, and *blue*.

adverb A word that gives more information about an adjective, verb, etc., saying when, where, how, e.g. *immediately*, *there*, *very*.

adverbial The part of the sentence that provides further information, usually about the verb, e.g. *carefully* in *They chose the site carefully.*

adverbial clause A subordinate clause introduced by a word such as *because, if, when, where,* and *while.*

adverbial phrase A phrase based on or around a main adverb, e.g. *as soon as possible; strangely enough.*

agent The doer of the action of a verb, e.g. *Hugh* in the passive sentence *The supper was cooked by Hugh.*

agreement (or **concord**) The correspondence that exists between two or more words or phrases that must have the same number, gender, etc., for the sentence to be grammatical, e.g. *She* and *has* in *She has a friend.*

apposition The relationship between two noun phrases that refer to exactly the same person or thing and define him, her, or it more closely, e.g. *Paris* and the *capital of France* in *Paris, the capital of France.*

appositive clause A clause which is attached to an abstract noun such as *belief, fact, knowledge,* or *suggestion,* and which indicates what is believed, known, suggested, etc., e.g. *the belief that God exists.*

article See **definite article; indefinite article.**

attributive adjective An adjective that comes before the noun it relates to, e.g. *red* in *a red dress.*

auxiliary verb A verb that is used in front of a main verb, e.g. *do, is, have, will, shall: I do sometimes make mistakes.*

back formation The process of forming a new word by removing the ending from another word, e.g. the verb *laze* from the adjective *lazy*.

case The form of a noun or pronoun that changes according to its use in a sentence, e.g. *Colin – Colin's, I – me*. See also **object case**; **possessive case**; **subject case**.

clause A group of words containing a subject and a finite verb which forms a whole sentence or part of one, e.g. *They still hope | that she'll come back* is a sentence containing two clauses.

collective noun A noun that refers to a group of people or things, e.g. *committee, crew, government, flock, herd, team*.

comment clause A short clause inserted into a sentence to show the speaker's attitude to what they are saying, e.g. *to be frank*, or *to put it another way*.

common noun A noun that is not a proper noun, e.g. *road, boy, happiness*.

comparative The form of an adjective used when making comparisons, e.g. *lighter, sweeter, more comfortable*. See also **superlative**.

comparative clause A type of subordinate clause that expresses a comparison between two or more things, e.g. *as long as I could* in *I waited as long as I could*.

complement The word or phrase that follows a linking verb (*be, seem, feel*, etc.). In *James is a computer expert*, the complement is *a computer expert*.

complex sentence A sentence consisting of a main clause and one or more subordinate clauses, e.g. *I can't come | because I'll be in London on Tuesday*.

compound sentence A multiple sentence consisting of two or more main clauses, linked together by *and*, *but*, or *or*, e.g. *Henry is a lorry driver and Jane works part-time in a supermarket*.

concord See **agreement**.

concrete noun A noun that refers to something that can be seen, touched, tasted, etc., e.g. *table* and *lion*. Compare **abstract noun**.

conjunction A word which connects other words, phrases, or clauses together, e.g. *and*, *or*, *while*. There are two types of conjunction: **coordinating conjunction** and **subordinating conjunction**.

consonant The sound represented by any of the letters *b*, *c*, *d*, *f*, *g*, *h*, *j*, *k*, *l*, *m*, *n*, *p*, *q*, *r*, *s*, *t*, *v*, *w*, *x*, *y*, and *z*.

continuous tense A tense of a verb that expresses actions that are going on, were going on, or will be going on at a particular time, constructed using *to be* together with the *-ing* form of the verb, e.g. *I am cooking*.

contraction 1 A word formed by shortening a word and attaching it to the word before it, e.g. *'re* for *are* in *you're*. **2** An abbreviation in which the first and final letters of the full form are retained, e.g. *Mr*, *Dr*.

coordinating conjunction A conjunction that links words, phrases, or clauses that have equal status, e.g. *and*, *or*, and *but*.

coordination The grammatical process of linking together elements of a sentence that have equal status, e.g. in the sentences *The day was fine | but rather chilly* and *James likes coffee, | but Henry prefers tea.*

countable noun A noun that can form a plural and can be preceded by *a* or *an*, e.g. *table, equivalent.* Compare **uncountable noun**.

dangling participle A participle that is wrongly or ambiguously placed, e.g. *blown to bits by the blast,* in *Blown to bits by the blast, workers were removing the rubble from the building.*

defining clause See **restrictive or defining clause**.

definite article The word *the.*

demonstrative pronouns The words *this, that, these,* and *those,* which point out or demonstrate which of a number of things are being referred to.

determiner A word that comes in front of and relates to a noun. Determiners specify the particular object or person, or the number of objects or persons, in a group that a noun refers to. They include *a, the, this, that, all, each, every, few, more, much, many, some, which, whichever,* and *what.*

diphthong The combination of two vowel sounds, e.g. the *a* sound in *hay* or *rain,* the *o* sound in *note* or *coat.*

directive An order or request to other people to do or to stop doing something, e.g. *Stop!*

direct object The word or phrase – usually a noun or pronoun – that is directly affected by the action of a verb, e.g. in *The car hit a tree,* the direct object is *a tree.*

direct speech The way of referring to the exact words that a person has used, e.g. *'I'm sorry, but I can't help you'* in *'I'm sorry, but I can't help you,' she said*. Compare **reported or indirect speech**.

double negative The use of two negatives in one sentence, e.g. *I don't owe you nothing*.

emphatic pronouns The pronouns which are the same in form as **reflexive pronouns** (*myself, himself,* etc.) and which usually follow immediately after the noun or pronoun they relate to, e.g. *myself* in *I myself have said as much*. Their function is to give emphasis.

exclamation An expression of surprise, approval, or annoyance, e.g. *What fun!*

feminine See **gender**.

finite clause A clause that contains a phrase with a **finite verb**, e.g. *I read the book*.

finite verb A verb that is used with a subject, in one of the tenses (past, present, etc.) and with an inflection that relates it to the subject, in contrast to an infinitive or a participle. E.g. *has* in *She has three children*.

first person Used to describe the pronouns *I* (singular) or *we* (plural) or the form of the verb used with *I* or *we*.

future tense The tense usually formed using the auxiliaries *will* or *shall*.

gender The classification of nouns and pronouns as masculine (e.g. *uncle, he*), feminine (e.g. *aunt, she*), or non-personal (neither masculine nor feminine, e.g. *it*).

genitive case See **possessive case**.

gradable Used to describe an adjective that can stand for a quality which can vary in degree, e.g. *young* in *a young person*. Compare **non-gradable**.

imperative mood The form of a verb that is used for giving orders, e.g. *Listen!*

indefinite article The words *a* and *an*.

indefinite pronouns Pronouns that refer to people or things without stating specifically who or what they are, e.g. *anyone*, *everybody*, *nobody*, *something*, *all*, *both*, *some*.

indicative mood The ordinary form of the verb used for making statements or asking questions. Compare **imperative mood**; **subjunctive mood**.

indirect object The additional object that occurs with some verbs that involve the action of giving, e.g. *me* in *He gave me a kiss*.

indirect speech See **reported or indirect speech**.

infinitive The base form of a verb that, in English, is often formed with *to*, e.g. *to come*, *to go*.

inflection A letter or letters added to the base form of a word to show its number, tense, person, etc. E.g. the inflection *-s* is added to the majority of nouns in English to form their plural; the inflections *-ing* and *-ed* are added to the base forms of most verbs to form their present and past participles respectively.

interjection One of a group of words that have the exclamatory function of expressing an emotion such as surprise, approval, anger, or pain: *ah!*, *oh!*, *ouch!*, *psst!*

interrogative adverbs Words that begin questions, e.g. *how*, *when*, and *where*.

interrogative pronouns Pronouns that begin questions: *who*, *whom*, *whose*, *what*, and *which*.

intonation The variation in pitch of the speaker's voice to show that they are asking a question, expressing surprise, etc. E.g. when asking a question, the pitch of the speaker's voice usually rises towards the end of the sentence.

intransitive verb A verb that does not have a direct object, e.g. *advanced* in *The army advanced*. Compare **transitive verb**.

invariable nouns A noun that is either always singular or always plural, e.g. *scissors*, *cattle*.

irregular Used to describe a word or form of a word that does not conform to a standard pattern. A verb is described as irregular if its past tense and past participle do not follow the standard pattern of adding *-ed* to the base form. Examples are: *come* (past tense *came*, past participle *come*); *drive* (past tense *drove*, past participle *driven*); *eat* (past tense *ate*, past participle *eaten*); *run* (past tense *ran*, past participle *run*); *see* (past tense *saw*, past participle *seen*). Regular nouns form their plural with *-s* or *-es*; the noun *child* is irregular because its plural form is *children*. Compare **regular**.

linking verb A verb such as *be*, *seem*, or *feel* that links the verb's subject with a complement, e.g. *is* in *James is a computer expert*.

main clause A clause that is complete in itself. Every major sentence must have at least one main clause, and a main clause on its own can constitute a sentence.

major sentence A sentence that contains a finite verb, e.g. *We drove to London*.

masculine See **gender**.

minor sentence A sentence that does not contain a finite verb, e.g. *Impossible!*

modifier A word which provides more information about other words and describes the things or people that they stand for more specifically, e.g. *car* in *car keys*.

mood A form of a verb: see **imperative mood**; **indicative mood**; and **subjunctive mood**.

multiple sentence A sentence with more than one clause, which may consist of more than one main clause or a main clause together with a number of subordinate clauses e.g. *Hugh writes books but Sandra is a sculptor*.

multi-word verb See **phrasal verb**.

non-defining clause See **non-restrictive clause**.

non-finite verb A form of the verb that is the infinitive (usually preceded by *to*, e.g. *to sing*), the present participle (e.g. *singing*), or the past participle (e.g. *sung*).

non-gradable Used to describe an adjective that cannot be used with such words as *very*, *slightly*, etc., e.g. *perfect*, *impossible*, *unique*. Compare **gradable**.

non-restrictive or non-defining clause A type of clause which contains information that is incidental and could be omitted from the sentence, e.g. *which comes halfway down the page* in *The paragraph, which comes halfway down the page, mentions you by name*. Compare **restrictive or defining clause**.

noun A word that stands for a thing, a person, or a quality, e.g. *instructor, happiness, Australia*.

noun phrase A group of related words, one of which is a noun or pronoun, e.g. *a child, a small child, a child with learning difficulties, a child who is of above average intelligence*.

object The word or phrase – usually a noun or pronoun – that is affected by the action of the verb and often comes after the verb, e.g. *a tree* in *The car hit a tree*. See also **direct object**; **indirect object**.

object case The form of a pronoun when used as the object of a sentence or when it follows a preposition, e.g. *me, them*.

participle See **past participle**; **present participle**.

passive Used to describe a verb in which the subject is affected by the action of the verb, e.g. *was cooked* in *The supper was cooked by Hugh*. Compare **active**.

past participle The form of a verb that is used to form the perfect tenses of verbs and the passive; in regular verbs, the *-ed* form of the verb, e.g. *cooked, exhausted*.

perfect tense A past tense of the verb formed with the auxiliary verb *have* together with the *-ed* form of a regular verb or the past participle of an irregular verb, e.g. *I have cooked, I had sung*.

person See **first person**; **second person**; **third person**.

personal pronoun A pronoun such as *I*, *you*, *her*, or *them*.

phrasal verb (or **multi-word verb**) A verb in which the base form is accompanied by an adverb or a preposition or both: *do down*, *do up*, *do away with*, usually with a distinct meaning that is not always deducible from its component parts, e.g. *do away with* means 'to get rid of'.

plural The form of a word used when it refers to more than one person or thing. *Cats* and *mice* are the plural forms of *cat* and *mouse* respectively, the former being regular, the latter irregular. Compare **singular**.

possessive case (or **genitive case**) The case or form of a noun or pronoun that is used to show possession, e.g. *Jill's* in *Jill's car*.

possessive pronoun Any of the personal pronouns *mine*, *yours*, *his*, *hers*, *its*, *ours*, and *theirs*.

postpositive adjective An adjective that is placed immediately after a noun or pronoun, e.g. *possible* in *everything possible*.

predicative adjective An adjective that is used after a verb such as *be*, *become*, or *seem*, e.g. *red* in *The dress is red*.

prefix A component that can be attached to the beginning of an existing word to change that word's meaning, e.g. *un* added to *happy* to give *unhappy*; *anti* added to *aircraft* to give *antiaircraft*.

preposition A word that is placed before other words, especially nouns, phrases, or clauses to link them into the sentence, e.g. *after*, *at*, *before*, *behind*, *for*, *in*, *of*, *out*.

present participle The form of a verb that is used to make the continuous forms of verbs; the *-ing* form of the verb, e.g. *cooking*.

pronoun A word that can replace a noun, e.g. *she, I, mine, themselves, these, both*. See also **demonstrative pronouns**; **emphatic pronouns**; **indefinite pronouns**; **interrogative pronouns**; **personal pronoun**; **possessive pronoun**; **reflexive pronouns**; **relative pronoun**.

proper noun A noun that denotes a specific person or thing, e.g. *Sam, Shakespeare, New York, October, Christmas, Marxism*.

question A type of sentence in which the speaker asks for information and usually expects a response, e.g. *How did you know?*

reflexive pronouns The words formed by adding *-self* (singular) or *-selves* (plural) to either the object or the possessive form of the personal pronoun: *myself, yourself, himself, itself, ourselves, yourselves*, and *themselves*. See also **emphatic pronouns**.

regular Used to describe a word or form of a word that conforms to the standard pattern. A verb is described as regular if its past tense and past participle are formed by adding *-ed* to the base form (or *-d* if the base form ends in *-e*): *cook – cooked; walk – walked; remember – remembered; arrive – arrived*. Nouns are described as regular if they form their plural with *-s* or *-es*. Compare **irregular**.

relative adverbs The words *when* and *where* used at the beginning of a relative clause.

relative clause A clause which gives more specific information about the noun that it follows and which begins with a word such as *that, which, who, whose, when*, or *where*. E.g. *that I lent you* in *the book that I lent you*.

relative pronoun The word *that, which, who, whom*, or *whose* when used to begin a relative clause.

reported clause The clause that gives the words that are spoken, e.g. *'I'm sorry, but I can't help you'* in *'I'm sorry, but I can't help you,' he said.*

reported or indirect speech The way of referring to what someone said without using inverted commas. In reported speech, the words that are spoken are integrated into the framework of the sentence, e.g. *She said that she was sorry.* Compare **direct speech**.

reporting clause The clause consisting of a subject and a verb of saying, e.g. *she said* in *'I'm sorry, but I can't help you,' she said.*

restrictive or defining clause A type of clause that contains essential information which identifies a particular person or thing. E.g. the clause *that mentions you by name* is a restrictive clause in the sentence *The paragraph that mentions you by name comes about halfway down the page.* Compare **non-restrictive or non-defining clause**.

second person Used to describe the pronoun *you* or the form of the verb used with *you*.

sentence A meaningful series of words, with a capital letter at the beginning and a full stop, a question mark, or an exclamation mark at the end.

singular The form of a word used when it refers to only one person or thing. Compare **plural**.

split infinitive An infinitive with a word or phrase placed between the *to* and the base form of the verb, e.g. *to sweetly sing*.

statement The commonest type of sentence, which begins with a capital letter, ends with a full stop, and presents the listener or reader with a piece of information without necessarily expecting any response from them, e.g. *My husband took the dog for a walk along the towpath.*

stress The additional force or volume given to a particular part of a word when it is spoken, e.g. the first syllable of *later* or the second syllable of *potato* when speaking these words.

subject The word or phrase – usually a noun or pronoun – that comes before the verb in an ordinary sentence. The subject says what the sentence is about: who or what carries out the action of the verb, e.g. in *The car hit a tree*, the subject is *The car*.

subject case The form of a pronoun used when it is the subject of a sentence, e.g. *I, we, he, she, they*.

subjunctive mood The form of a verb that is sometimes used in clauses expressing a wish, demand, or recommendation, e.g. *give* in *I suggest she give it more thought*. Compare **imperative mood**; **indicative mood**.

subordinate clause A clause that is incomplete in itself and cannot stand by itself, e.g. *because I was afraid of being late* in *I ran all the way because I was afraid of being late.*

subordinating conjunction A conjunction that links parts of a sentence that do not have equal status, e.g. *after* in *I found out after she had left the company.*

suffix A component that is added to the end of a word to change that word's meaning, e.g. *-ly* added to the adjective *brief* to give the adverb *briefly*.

superlative The form of adjective that is used to show that a thing possesses a quality to a greater degree than two or more other things, e.g. *sweetest, most comfortable*. See also **comparative**.

tag question A statement with a little tag tacked on at the end, e.g. *is it?* in *It isn't time to go yet, is it?*

tense The form of a verb that relates to a time frame within which the action of the verb takes place, e.g. the present tense refers to action taking place now: *I cook, we are cooking*.

third person Used to describe the singular pronouns *he, she, it* or the plural *they* or the forms of the verb used with them.

transitive verb A verb that has a direct object, e.g. *bring* in *bring some food to the party*. Compare **intransitive verb**.

uncountable noun A noun that does not normally form a plural and cannot normally be preceded by *a* or *an*, e.g. *mud, rice, happiness*. Compare **countable noun**.

variable noun A noun that changes its form in the plural, e.g. *flower – flowers; mouse – mice*.

verb A word that stands for an action, e.g. *kick, spend, spat, hurt*.

voice See **active**; **passive**.

vowel The sound represented by any of the letters *a, e, i, o, u*, and sometimes *y*.

zero plural A noun whose form does not change whether it is singular or plural, e.g. *sheep*.